To Harry —

My best wishes

Pollyanne

Pickering

# On Top

ᐊᐳᑦ OF ᐊᐳᑦ

# The World

On Top of the World

# On Top of The World

Pollyanna Pickering

text and photography by

Anna-Louise Pickering

foreword by Brigitte Bardot

preface by Billy Connolly

Otter House (Licensing) Limited

*In memory of my father*
*Ken Pickering*

First published in Great Britain in 2001 by
Otter House (Licensing) Limited,
Water Lane, Haven Banks, Exeter EX2 8BY



Designed by Sue Stainton and Rosemary Lee

British Library Cataloguing in Publication Data
A catalogue record for this book is available from the British Library.

ISBN 0 9529 369 2 5



Colour reproduction by Peninsular Services, Exeter, Devon
Printed and bound in Hong Kong through Printworks International Ltd

# Foreword

Je ne connais pas Pollyanna, mais j'ai découvert son talent avec :
« GIANT PANDAS AND SLEEPING DRAGONS »
nous avons un point commun qui est l'amour des animaux et un regard naïf et admiratif pour la nature.
Cette merveilleuse photographe, douée d'un talent exceptionnel de peintre m'a entraînée dans un voyage inoubliable plein de poésie dans la Chine des pandas aux grands yeux tristes et aux corps de peluche, m'a fait découvrir une face cachée de ce pays qui comme elle le dit si bien est partagé entre le ying et le yang —
C'est pourquoi j'ai accepté avec fierté d'écrire cette petite préface pour "ON TOP of the WORLD" que je découvrirai en même temps que vous, avec j'en suis sûre autant d'émerveillement que pour le précédent.
— St Exupery a dit : "On ne voit bien qu'avec le coeur, l'essentiel est invisible pour les yeux"
Merci Pollyanna et aussi Bravo à Anne Louise qui écrit de si beaux textes ! —

juin 2001. Brigitte Bardot

I did not know of Pollyanna until I discovered her talent in the book *'Giant Pandas and Sleeping Dragons'*. We share a common love of animals, and are naive and full of admiration in the way we look at the natural world. The marvellous photographer, Anna-Louise, along with a painter gifted with an exceptional artistic talent, have transported me on an unforgettable journey, full of poetry, into the China of the Giant Pandas, which look like teddy bears with their huge, sad eyes. The book also helped me to discover a hidden face of this country which, as Pollyanna says so well, is divided between the Yin and the Yang.

That is why I am proud to write this short foreword for *'On Top of the World'*, a book which I will discover at the same time as you, the reader, and I am sure with as much amazement as the one which preceded it.

St Expury said "One only sees with the heart - the essential is invisible to the eyes". Thank you Pollyanna, and also congratulations to Anna-Louise who has written such a beautiful book.

**Brigitte Bardot**
June 2001

*"Ahead lies adventure and the unknown, a route never before explored…
a new world seems to open, and a new kind of adaptation...
when I travel I make my best meditations."*

Father George Carson O M I
Arctic Missionary

# Preface

*Billy Connolly has kindly let us use extracts from his Arctic Diaries as a preface to 'On Top of the World'*

## A Scot in the Arctic

I'VE never been so alone before, sitting on top of the world, in a tent, pitched on the sea. If you ever get the chance, whatever the circumstances, get yourself to the Arctic. It's breathtaking to say the least. Serene, I think is the word. It's bigger, it's been there longer, and it knows more about itself than you are ever likely to learn. And so it enforces a kind of humility on you.

There's a silence as soon as you're about a mile onto the ice that you could cut with a knife. You can almost hear it. There's a soft, all enveloping feel to it - it's extraordinary in its density. For that alone, this place is worth a visit.

Very few men on earth - or women for that matter - have had a chance to ride through the Arctic in a dog sleigh. It's absolutely beautiful, especially when there are no skidoos or motorised vehicles around you. When you're out there on the virgin snow, and it's just you and the dogs swishing along - it's very nice indeed - except dogs do smell a bit.

Incidentally, have you wondered how I went to the bathroom? Has it crossed your mind? Or maybe you don't think stuff like that. Yes you do. You wonder how to go to the bathroom in sub-zero temperatures. Well I'm not telling you. But I had to bare my bum to the elements and it wasn't easy. You have to be quick and learned. But to be quite frank that was one of my main worries before I made the trip. I read the SAS survival book and it says in severely low temperatures it's best to do it in the tent and use the heat. I thought, 'Not this soldier. I'll just be a wee bit colder, and risk frostbite on the bum'.

But the Arctic is very, very hard. Being there was harder than anything I've ever done, with the wind howling so cold it would halve you in two. My thought processes were strange and frightening sometimes, as my mind wandered a wee bit. I fantasised a lot. It was very odd out on the sea, like you're the only person on the whole planet, or the man on the moon or something. It really is extraordinary . . . I wasn't even sure if I liked it.

The strangest thing is, I wasn't frightened. You don't feel the fear you think you will. You just think a lot about the bigness of things, and this emptiness that isn't actually empty. There's a presence which is just breathtaking. My experiences of the Arctic reminded me that the world is an unbelievably great place.

# Contents

Pollyanna and Anna-Louise: You Have Been Warned!

WHEN we returned from our expedition into the Arctic, there were two questions to which all of our friends wanted to know the answers. The first was "what did you have to wear to survive temperatures as low as –40°C?" This was always swiftly followed by "and how did you go to the loo?" The first subject will be covered in detail in the diaries of our journey. The second question can be answered in one word.

Quickly.

Before we set out on our journey, the question we were most frequently asked was also very short - "Why?" This question, too, was not difficult to answer. Pollyanna had embarked four years earlier on a series of journeys to study and paint endangered and threatened species in their natural habitat. She had already travelled through Africa and India, journeys that had resulted in acclaimed exhibitions of portraits of big cats and exotic wildlife. For several months she had been contemplating a journey to a contrasting habitat - the Arctic home of the polar bear. By sharing and experiencing first hand these remote areas she is able to portray wildlife in a uniquely compelling way, bringing a beauty and reality to her paintings which cannot be captured in any other way.

But behind the deceptively short query, lay the real question - "Whatever are you thinking of, don't you know that it will be COLD up there, polar bears are big and dangerous, do you really think you will come back ALIVE?" Our advisors had a valid point. On the face of it we were the two least eligible Arctic explorers ever to apply for the job. Your average polar adventurer is tall, bearded, butch, rugged and at the peak of physical fitness. I am tall.

Blithely ignoring these minor concerns, I began researching suitable areas to visit, and in the spring of 1991 we found ourselves On Top of The World.

*Anna-Louise Pickering*

# THE JOURNEY

eyes watchful / black

fur extremely dense
almost apricot shading
to creamy white

deep indigo in
shadows

ice throws back
reflected light onto
under fur

Study of a Polar bear —

Pollyanna Pickering

*Chapter One*

*"Men wanted for hazardous journey. Small wages, bitter cold, long months of complete darkness, safe return doubtful. Honour and recognition in case of success."*

ADVERT PLACED BY SIR ERNEST SHACKLETON

IF you nip into your local travel agent and announce that you would like to book a trip into a remote area of wilderness above the Arctic Circle, where there may be a possibility of seeing wild polar bears as they roam the ice floes, you are likely to be met with strange looks and nervous laughter.

Before setting out on an expedition we spend many months researching the best area to explore. Polar bears live throughout the Arctic region. We needed to find an area that was relatively accessible, where we could hire local people willing to guide us through the inhospitable terrain, and where there would be the greatest chance of finding the bears. The Arctic is owned by five nations: Russia, Norway, Greenland, Canada and the United States of America. We decided early on to head for the Canadian Arctic for several very practical reasons, not least the lack of visa restrictions and the widespread use of the English language. The obvious choice of destination was the town of Churchill on the Hudson Bay. Churchill has gained an international reputation as the town built on a polar bear migration route. Each autumn bears gather in great numbers waiting for Hudson Bay to freeze over. A healthy tourist industry has sprung up as wildlife enthusiasts travel out into the frozen landscape to see the bears at close quarters.

Although we were keen to visit this unique town, we ruled it out as our first destination for a variety of reasons. In recent years successful measures have been implemented to keep the bears away from the town's rubbish dumps. At the time we were planning the journey the bears could be seen scavenging through the detritus and trash produced by the community. Pollyanna could not visualise sketching the bears as they chewed playfully on old tyres and discarded packaging. Churchill lies just below the Arctic Circle, on the edge of the tree line, so even away from the site of the tip, the bears are most frequently seen sitting in amongst branches of stunted willows. The town's relatively southerly position also means that when the

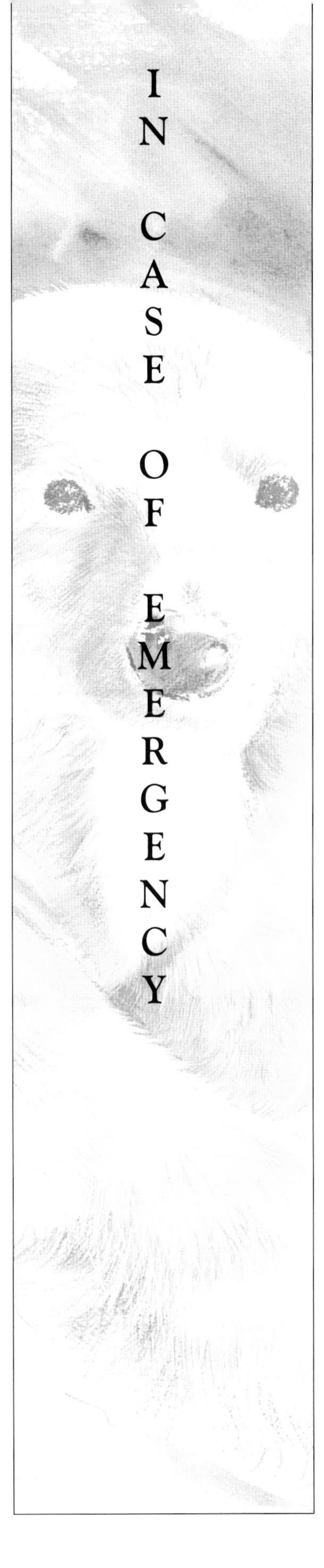

NEVER ONE TO TRAVEL LIGHT . . .

bears are present there is a fair chance that the weather will be too warm for snow. Our plans to visit Churchill were, therefore, temporarily shelved.

Pollyanna had visions of painting polar bears within the Arctic wilderness - glittering expanses of snow untainted even by trees. And, incidentally, by any human constructions, including desirable ones such as emergency medical facilities, or hotels with room service and heated swimming pools.

Further research and discussions with specialist travel companies, naturalists and wildlife photographers eventually lead us to settle on a destination. Below the tip of Baffin Island, a rugged land of mountains and glaciers, lies a small community rejoicing in the name of Igloolik. The majority of native Inuit people in the area still live in the traditional way, driving dog sleds out on to the ice, and hunting for food. They are familiar with travelling in a region that remains wilderness and with the areas in which the seals, caribou and polar bears are most likely to be found. However, as well as housing a community of Inuit people, Igloolik is a stopping-off point for Canadian construction workers employed in the oil fields and mines which provide the majority of the income in the Northwest Territories, exploiting the rich mineral resources of the Arctic region. This means that we can 'hitch a lift' north on a plane carrying workers and supplies out to the ice floes and arrive at a northerly point relatively quickly. An American travel company, Canada North Outfitting inc., sensibly based in the warmer climes of Florida, is able to arrange our flights and make initial contact with two people in the community who will act as our guides in our search for the ice bears.

A VERITABLE MOUNTAIN OF CLOTHING.

With all the necessary travel arrangements in place, we turn our attentions to other pressing problems - our luggage, and ourselves. Never one to travel light at the best of times, prior to this journey I found myself facing a veritable mountain of clothing and equipment. Thermal underwear, fleece leggings and sweaters, padded jackets, waterproofs and mummy-style sleeping bags (guaranteed to sustain life in temperatures of –80°C) were topped with army surplus bedding rolls. Jostling for space were my cameras, lenses, filters, films and notebooks.

Added to Pollyanna's not inconsiderable supplies of sketching equipment - paints, brushes, drawing-board, loose sheets of papers, sketch pads, pencils, oil pastels - we soon found we had filled between us two cases, two large canvas bags (with the sleeping rolls tied on top) two camera bags, two flight bags and one case of art materials. It was starting to look as though we would need to charter our own plane to reach Igloolik. (In the end the most nightmarish part of the entire 4,260 km journey from home to the Arctic turned out to be trying to manage our luggage on the London underground!)

Taking up a large portion of my suitcase is my legendary first-aid kit. Initially devised to deal with any emergency which may befall us whilst staying in a remote African village, our supplies of ointments, bandages, pills and potions had to be supplemented with a few specialist items, such as waterproof matches and hand warmers to thaw out frozen fingers – I even invest in a Swiss army knife to encourage that authentic explorer feeling. In pride of place, neatly vacuum packed into plastic pouches, are thin silver blankets, as modelled by collapsing runners at the end of the London Marathon. Apparently, the blurb reassures us 'in case of emergency' they would help us to maintain body temperature in even the most extreme of conditions. Quite what sort of emergency was gong to result in me stranded in the middle of the Arctic wasteland wrapped in a large piece of tin foil was something that I preferred not to contemplate.

We were not planning to be explorers in the true sense of the word because the area we were hoping to visit was on the edge of human habitation and we would not be covering new previously uncharted ground (unless the plans went seriously awry!). Nor were we heading for the North Pole, or attempting to circumnavigate the Arctic Circle on foot. Nevertheless, it was clear that a certain level of fitness would be required. So, how best to train for weeks of physical discomfort in a frozen wilderness? Naturally by booking into the cosseted warmth of a luxurious English health farm. And so it was that the highly trained gym instructors at Hoar Cross Hall in Staffordshire, lead by former aerobics champion Micah Hudson, embarked on the not insignificant task of shaping my pale and scrawny frame into a taut muscular machine capable of hiking miles through the snow. My initial fitness tests indicated that at this stage it would probably be unwise to tackle a long flight of stairs without a medical team on standby, but faithfully following the exercise routine devised for me meant that, by the time our departure date arrived, I could lift my camera bag unaided.

One thing the comfortable surroundings of the health farm could not prepare us for was

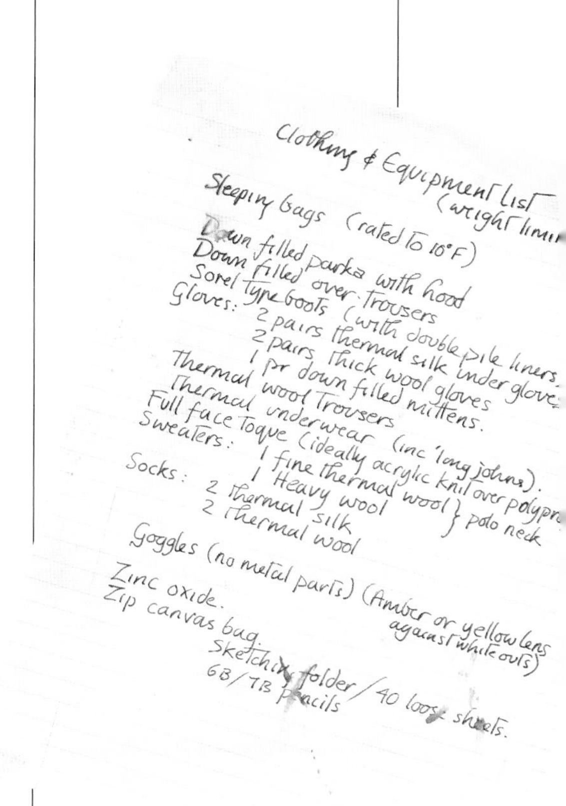

Clothing & Equipment list
(weight limi

Sleeping bags (rated to 10°F)

Down filled parka with hood
Down filled over-trousers
Sorel type boots (with double pile liners.
Gloves: 2 pairs thermal silk under gloves
2 pairs thick wool gloves
1 pr down filled mittens.
Thermal wool trousers
Thermal underwear (inc 'long johns).
Full face toque (ideally acrylic knit over polypr
Sweaters: 1 fine thermal wool } polo neck
1 Heavy wool
Socks: 2 thermal silk
2 thermal wool

Goggles (no metal parts) (Amber or yellow lens against whiteouts)

Zinc oxide.
Zip canvas bag.
Sketching folder / 40 loose sheets.
6B/7B Pencils

Clothing and equipment list.

With Aerobics champion Micah.

the rigours of sleeping in tents on the ice floes. Having never been possessed of a particularly outward-bound mentality, I had managed to reach the age of twenty-one without spending a night under canvas. Horrified acquaintances volunteered the use of a bewildering assortment of tents, urging me to spend a few nights sleeping on the lawn by way of rehearsal. Madness. Sleeping in an English country garden in February? I would never survive until the morning. I had no intention of giving up my electric blanket until it became absolutely necessary.

As we gradually became fitter, the mountain of packing grew ever higher and, as the date of departure loomed nearer, the more people began to regale us with horror stories of adventurers who had set out with cheerful determination to conquer the Arctic, never to return. We listened with increasing trepidation to tales of explorers lost in blizzards, travelling in ever decreasing circles before perishing in the wilderness; of the German scientist who woke in the middle of the night to the screams of one of his colleagues being eaten alive by the polar bear who had ripped his way through the canvas wall of his tent; of those who had returned alive but lacking fingers, toes, noses, all lost to the vicious grip of frostbite - or physically intact, but rambling and incoherent, driven insane by the unimaginable vastness of the white horizon.

Pollyanna - an unlikely Arctic explorer

Outlaw
In the collection of Mr and Mrs Sparkes (UK)

*Chapter Two*

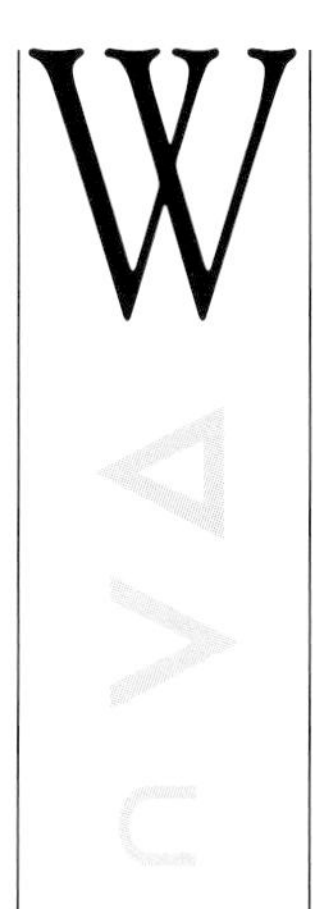

WE anticipated that our time in the Arctic would be fairly gruelling, so we made plans to recover from the transatlantic flights, and get our internal clocks fully adjusted to the six-hour time difference, before the tough part of our journey began. In reality these plans became a lovely excuse to fly to Toronto, hire a car, and take a week to drive up the eastern coast of Canada to Ottawa, the departure point for our first internal flight.

On arrival at Toronto airport, our luggage teetering precariously on a trolley, we present ourselves at the car hire desk. The girl behind the desk taps our booking reference into a computer and announces that we have been allocated a Sierra. We are escorted down to the hire car garage, where the representative leans on the bonnet of a huge gleaming black vehicle while he completes the paperwork. We sign on the dotted line, accept the key and his wishes for both a pleasant stay in Canada and a nice day, and wait to be shown to our car. A short while later we are still waiting. Eventually I break the increasingly awkward silence and ask where exactly our car can be found. Baffled, our rep pats the bonnet of the car he had been using as an impromptu desk. Our hire car is so large I had failed to see it.

In my jet-lagged mind I had heard Sierra and thought Ford. In fact the rep had said Ciera and meant Oldsmobile. To be precise, an Oldsmobile Cutlass Ciera, which needed returning to the depot in Ottawa. As we were only driving one way the job was ours. It was love at first drive. My heart broke a little when we finally had to leave our smooth, sleek, comfortable car in the return park at Ottawa airport, albeit by that stage mud splattered both inside and out.

Fully equipped with transport, we set out on our epic journey north by driving south. Before leaving England we had made contact with a charming lady named Kay McKeever, founder of the Owl Rehabilitation Foundation, based in Vineland, a small town just north of Niagara. Although her facility was not normally open to the public, she had kindly agreed that we could visit.

We arrive at coffee time, to find ourselves gatecrashing a party. Kay's husband Larry is celebrating his eighty-fifth birthday, sharing a cake iced in vivid pink lettering with Kay and all

Love at first drive.

The Owl Rehabilitation Foundation.

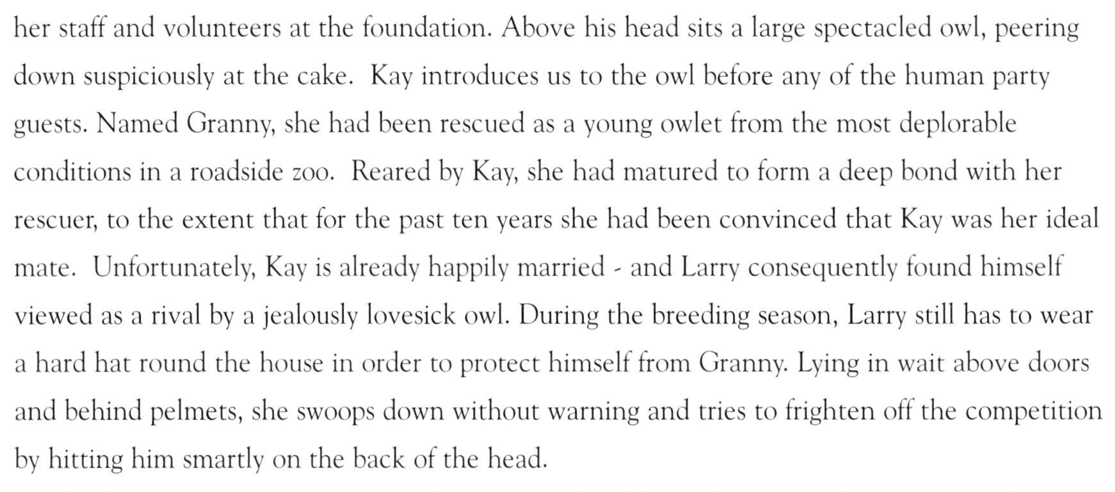

her staff and volunteers at the foundation. Above his head sits a large spectacled owl, peering down suspiciously at the cake. Kay introduces us to the owl before any of the human party guests. Named Granny, she had been rescued as a young owlet from the most deplorable conditions in a roadside zoo. Reared by Kay, she had matured to form a deep bond with her rescuer, to the extent that for the past ten years she had been convinced that Kay was her ideal mate. Unfortunately, Kay is already happily married - and Larry consequently found himself viewed as a rival by a jealously lovesick owl. During the breeding season, Larry still has to wear a hard hat round the house in order to protect himself from Granny. Lying in wait above doors and behind pelmets, she swoops down without warning and tries to frighten off the competition by hitting him smartly on the back of the head.

The human guests are subsequently introduced as Mary-Ellen, Kip, Hugh, Steve and Rosie, and we join the celebrations as Larry continues to entertain us with reminiscences of his years with Kay. Since their marriage in 1967, he has loyally supported all her rescue work and grown used to sharing his life and his home with feathered patients - even his bedroom is not a safe refuge! One morning Kay awoke before Larry to find one of the young owlets, whom she had been hand feeding at regular intervals through the night, inching his way up the bedspread, all the while staring intently at Larry's mouth. Moments later Kay is flung forcibly out of bed, along with blankets bedding and pillows, as Larry wakes with a scream to find an owlet attached to his top lip. The young owl's very first attempt at hunting has resulted in the successful capture of Larry's moustache, which he has mistaken for a small furry rodent.

Kay introduces us to Granny.

We leave Larry to finish his cake in peace, as Kay leads us on a guided tour of her aviaries. She has every species of North American owl in her care. Most are temporary residents, orphaned youngsters, or injured adults who will be re-released into the wild at the earliest opportunity. A few are permanent residents - owls who have injuries that have left them with permanent disabilities making it impossible to fend for themselves in the wild. Kay has pioneered a wonderful fostering method of care in her hospital, having discovered that both male and female owls will respond to the "feed me" calls of baby owls - even when they are not their own young. In this way the owlets can be reared entirely by their own species, without human contact and then released into the wild without becoming imprinted on their human carers.

In order to feed her ever-increasing colony of owls, Kay has established a mouse-breeding programme. This ensures a constant supply of a food that is as natural as possible. She recounts a tale from her early days of running the foundation. A friend of a friend had a contact who bred guinea pigs for use in laboratory experiments. He would be happy to supply Kay with some of the pigs as free food for her owls. Although a little squeamish at the idea of using guinea pigs as dinner, Kay knows that they will be an ideal source of nutrition, and money is tight so she accepts. In due course a box arrives, containing a dozen guinea pigs. Kay cautiously peers in. The guinea pigs peer back. They are alive. This was not expected. How, as an animal lover, can she bring herself to kill them? Several phone calls later, Kay is advised that the most humane way would be to put them in a sack and secure the end around the exhaust pipe of her car, turning the engine on, thus gassing them quite painlessly with carbon monoxide. The deed is carried out and the dead guineas are placed in the aviaries of the largest owls. Kay returns to the house, having firmly decided that she will not be accepting another gift like this - there is no such thing as a free lunch, even for an owl. Moments later one of her volunteers comes running into the house. The guinea pigs have come back to life! They are moving! It's a miracle! Kay runs back to the aviary to find several very groggy guineas staggering round the aviaries, being watched doubtfully by owls, uncertain about prey larger than their usual mice and voles. Clearly the fumes had knocked the pigs unconscious and now, back in the fresh air, they are recovering. Having 'killed' them once, Kay cannot bring herself to carry out the deed a second time and so twelve guinea pigs spend a week scampering around the aviaries, before burrowing underneath the netting and escaping, to establish a new home on the banks of the river which runs through the sanctuary. A small colony still survives there to this day.

With or without guinea pigs, we are highly impressed by the foundation. Each aviary contains trees and bushes, providing the owls with 'safe' areas where they can hide from view if

MANY OF THE PENS ARE COVERED BY CCTV.

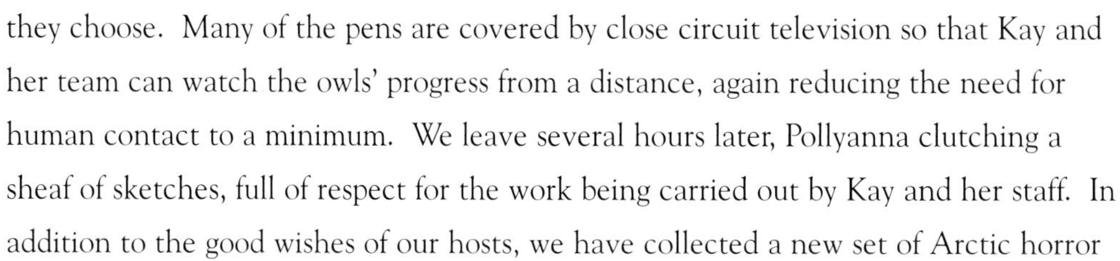

they choose. Many of the pens are covered by close circuit television so that Kay and her team can watch the owls' progress from a distance, again reducing the need for human contact to a minimum. We leave several hours later, Pollyanna clutching a sheaf of sketches, full of respect for the work being carried out by Kay and her staff. In addition to the good wishes of our hosts, we have collected a new set of Arctic horror stories, and dire warnings - this time including the welcome news that we may arrive in the Arctic just as the spring weather is getting warm enough for the annual mosquito hatch. I am hoping that 'mosquito hatch' is a quaint name for an annual local festival that involves much feasting and merriment, but no. Apparently, when spring arrives the temperatures rise above freezing for the first time in months and the mild weather brings with it a plague of mosquitoes, in places so dense that local residents cannot leave their homes. People have been known to die from the number of bites received. In the Arctic insects spend the winter months in a kind of suspended animation – producing within their bodies a glycerol-like 'anti-freeze' so effective that they can survive temperatures as low as –70°C unharmed. Unfortunately, we mere humans do not have this ability. Kay and Larry kindly donate another addition to the first-aid kit - a pot of mosquito repellent, guaranteed to repel anything within a three-mile radius. I sniff gingerly at the yellow, waxy contents and replace the lid, eyes watering. For the first time since we began planning the journey I am hoping for cold weather.

SINCE WE ARRIVED THERE HAS BEEN NO LET-UP IN THE RAIN.

Our drive north begins. We follow the shore of Lake Ontario, driving at times on the major 401 highway and where possible on the smaller back roads. There is water everywhere - the expanses of the lake, surrounded by soggy marshland, rivers, streams and impressively large ponds held back by solidly constructed beaver dams. Most of the time water is also pouring from the heavens. Since we arrived there has been no let-up in the rain, just an occasional patch of light drizzle to lift our spirits before the downpour resumes.

CANADIAN ROBIN.

We drive steadily onwards, stopping at every wildlife reserve that appears on our map. The Canadians worryingly refer to these areas as 'preserves', leading to images of squirrels pickled in aspic. Braving the rain we are delighted to see a wealth of native wildlife:

chipmunks, squirrels, both grey and strikingly jet black, and groundhogs, known locally as the woodchuck. Pollyanna is in her element and we sit quietly for hours as she sketches the chipmunks darting out from the trees and rocks. A huge country with a population less than that of London, Canada appears to us to be one huge nature preserve.

We have not made any hotel bookings in advance, preferring to drive at our own pace each day finding a room in the nearest town as we stop for the night. As we are well outside the main tourist season, we do not anticipate any problems in finding accommodation. Until we arrive in Belville on a Friday night that is. Every hotel is booked solid. We drive on to Odessa. Again we are turned away at the reception desk, back out into the rain to try our luck elsewhere. Until this point we had not been aware of the Canadian love of weekend conventions. Every room in every town is booked for two nights by members of various societies converging for two days of lectures, meetings and socialising with like-minded enthusiasts. Eventually we drip pathetically across the lobby of the Ambassador Hotel in Kingston. We are viewed with suspicion by the receptionist. Judging by appearances, we clearly cannot afford a room and, furthermore, if allowed in we will obviously steal the sheets, towels and cutlery before departing. Against her better judgement she grants us her last available room. The rest of the hotel has been occupied by the Ontario Catholic Women's Association and the restaurant is entirely full of immaculately coiffured ladies in smart suits, nametags pinned firmly to their lapels. Nameless, and with dripping hair, clothes muddied from a day stalking chipmunks and ground squirrels in the preserves, we feel we are not blending in successfully. We retreat and end up eating in the optimistically named Garden Café - in fact a few Formica tables set at the edge of the swimming pool where the air is pervaded with a powerful smell of chlorine and the ear-shattering screeches of small children enjoying themselves.

Exhausted by a day driving and an evening spent searching for accommodation, I collapse gratefully into my comfortable bed. I awake two hours later to find myself still horizontal, but three feet above the bed. The fire alarm has gone off. The nerve destroying sirens stop. Ears ringing I collapse back on the bed and clutch the sides of the mattress gasping for breath. My heart rate gradually slows until it drops back to a rate slightly lower than that of a nervous

Jet black squirrel

STUDY OF A RACOON
IN THE COLLECTION OF
MRS AND MRS HOLAH (UK)

hummingbird. All is quiet. Confident it was just a false alarm, I drift gently back to sleep. Twenty minutes later the alarm sounds again. This necessitates getting out of bed. I stagger across the room and peer blearily at the 'What to do in case of fire' instructions pinned to the door. 'In case of an intermittent alarm prepare to evacuate'. Is once every half hour intermittent? Does this call for clothes? Make up? Pollyanna starts gathering her sketches, while I 'phone reception. False alarm. Thank you.

7.00 am. I wake six inches above the bed, heart pounding, etc. The hotel alarm call consists of automatically switching the television on at full volume, while simultaneously ringing the 'phone which is five inches away from my ear, just in case any of the dead may not have been woken by 'Good Morning Canada' at decibel levels usually associated with a rock festival.

Fully rested, we drive on northwards. Our first stop is a small wildlife centre at Springwater. As the rain is still teeming down, we have the place practically to ourselves and we fall into conversation with one of the keepers. John is caring for two orphaned racoon cubs, their tiny black hands clutch at the feeding bottle of milk and their eyes screw up with pleasure as they greedily drink. We meet other residents, including adult racoons, outlaw bandits with black masks across their eyes. Pollyanna takes the opportunity to make a few quick sketches, though the rain splashing on to her paper causes her watercolour pencils to smudge and run as

CHIPMUNKS WITH EVERYTHING
IN THE COLLECTION OF MR AND MRS CLARKE (UK)

she tries to work. Even these quick studies will provide her with enough reference for the basis of a painting when she returns home to the studio. As the centre is so very quiet, John is happy to lead us out to a nearby area where he has been observing a den of wild foxes for several months. He points out the main entrance to the den and then returns to his duties at Springwater, leaving us to watch for any movements. He is fairly sure that the pair of foxes who have made their home here have cubs, but as yet he has not seen them. The rain has subsided to a light drizzle, so we settle ourselves quietly in the shelter of the trees and prepare for a long vigil. Many years of experience of looking for animals in the wild, both at home and on safari abroad, have taught us that the majority of wildlife watching trips consist of staring fixedly at a tree, a nest, the entrance to a den, or out across an empty prairie for several hours, waiting for an animal or bird to appear. If luck is with us, this is followed by a few minutes of frantic sketching and photography; or if not, by the drive home, sketch pad still pristine and unmarked.

On this occasion, however, I have no sooner unpacked my camera, when a black nose appears in the entrance to the den, dug into the earth beside the outlet of an old storm drain, and a red fox emerges into the open air, shaking the sandy earth from her coat. Canadian red foxes are classified as the same species as our European red fox, but she appears very different. Her coat is very thick, her fur being much longer and heavier than that of her British cousin and, in contrast, her black legs look longer and thinner. She stretches and walks around the den area apparently oblivious to the human presence, sniffing the ground, pausing and cocking her head on one side, presumably listening to small sounds from the woodland, inaudible to our ears. She lies down briefly, but is soon restlessly walking in front of her den again. Pollyanna is able to complete several sheets of sketches, her quick pencil strokes augmented with pastels to capture the deep glowing russet of the fur, before the fox disappears back into her underground lair. We wait for her to reappear. And wait. And wait. This is more familiar. Eventually we decide it is time to pack up our equipment and leave. We have been incredibly lucky to see the fox for such a length of time; the light is starting to fail and the rain, which has held off for a couple of hours, is threatening to return. Pollyanna collects together her

Pollyanna is able to complete several sheets of sketches, her quick pencil strokes augmented with pastels to capture the deep glowing russet of the fur, before the fox disappears.

A red fox emerges shaking the sandy earth from her coat.

THE CUBS EXPLORE THE OUTSIDE WORLD.

papers, watercolours, pencils and turns to go. I am still sorting my cameras - changing a lens, and replacing a film - when a movement catches my eye. A small head pops out of a second entrance to the den, a few yards behind the main hole where we have been focusing our attention. I make a small, unidentified strangled noise to try and attract Pollyanna's attention, without frightening away the tiny fox cub which has now ventured all the way out into the wide world above ground. Pollyanna quickly and quietly opens her sketch folder, as a second cub is followed by a third. The cubs are very small, dark brown with tiny tails just tipped with white. They explore cautiously, blinking their blue eyes in the daylight, stumbling on their still unsteady legs. Now we are oblivious to the darkening clouds, and even as the first few drops of rain start to threaten Pollyanna's sketches, we watch entranced as the adult fox re-emerges to keep a watchful eye on her young as they tumble and play.

We are starting to lose the light completely, but are reluctant to leave the fox cubs,

'BRAVE NEW WORLD'
DONATED TO WILDAID ANIMAL RESCUE.

when their mother makes the decision for us, gently nudging her young charges back into the tunnel and the safety of the den. We swiftly gather our belongings and start to make our way back to the car, parked on the edge of the woodland. A vivid flash of forked lightning illuminates the sky, followed almost immediately by a deep rumble of thunder. This is not good. When we have to walk any distance on foot we load our camera bags and art materials on to a luggage trolley, as the bags are too heavy to carry for any length of time. We have learnt this the hard way with pulled shoulders and strained back muscles. We now find ourselves in the middle of a wood, holding a metal trolley, while lightning forks through the sky at regular intervals. Pollyanna seizes the handle of the trolley - she has lived longer than me, if anyone is going to be struck by lightning it should be her. I protest that there is no logic whatsoever to this argument and wrestle the handle back, and we thus squabble our way back to the car, until drenched by the downpour we reach the safety of our vehicle, with its four comforting rubber tyres.

As we follow the coastline north, we fall into the habit of stopping in the early morning to buy sandwiches and snacks so that we can stop and eat whenever we are ready. Often, when using designated picnic areas, we find that the roles are temporarily reversed and the Canadian wildlife is watching us. Squirrels scamper down from trees in the hope of crumbs and on one occasion as we leave our table a racoon darts to the nearby litterbin and then scampers off clutching a prized apple core in his dextrous front paws. One lunchtime we park up close to an attractive stretch of water and sit down on the grass to eat our provisions. Travelling independently in this way brings with it many benefits, but also some disadvantages. On the plus side we are free to stop when and wherever we choose and then move on when we are ready. Pollyanna can spend an hour sketching a dead tree without holding up a restless group eager to drive on. The down side consists of a fair amount of time spent peering at maps muttering 'there should be a left turn here somewhere' - and of course with no one to point them out, sometimes the most obvious things go unnoticed. Thus we spend our lunch break idly wondering who has stuck neatly cut fence posts at seemingly random intervals around an area of marshland; it is not until I am chewing on the last mouthful of sandwich that the penny drops. The fence posts are, of course, the remains of small trees neatly felled by

BLACK BEAUTY
IN THE COLLECTION OF
MR AND MRS CHARLESWORTHY
(UK)

Small trees neatly felled by industrious beavers.

industrious beavers and then pulled away to be used in the construction of a dam. A short walk following the path of a narrow brook leads us to the construction site - an impressive wall of branches, stuffed with leaves and mud is holding back an expanse of still water. Pollyanna makes her way quietly and cautiously to the water's edge, looking carefully for any signs of life. I am rewarded with a brief glimpse of a beaver running at full speed in the opposite direction, before slipping gracefully into the water and diving out of sight.

Arriving in Ottawa, we have a free half-day to pass before our first internal flight. We decide to visit the Natural History Museum, which also boasts dioramas depicting traditional Native American and Inuit life. In the hope that viewing small groups of shop window

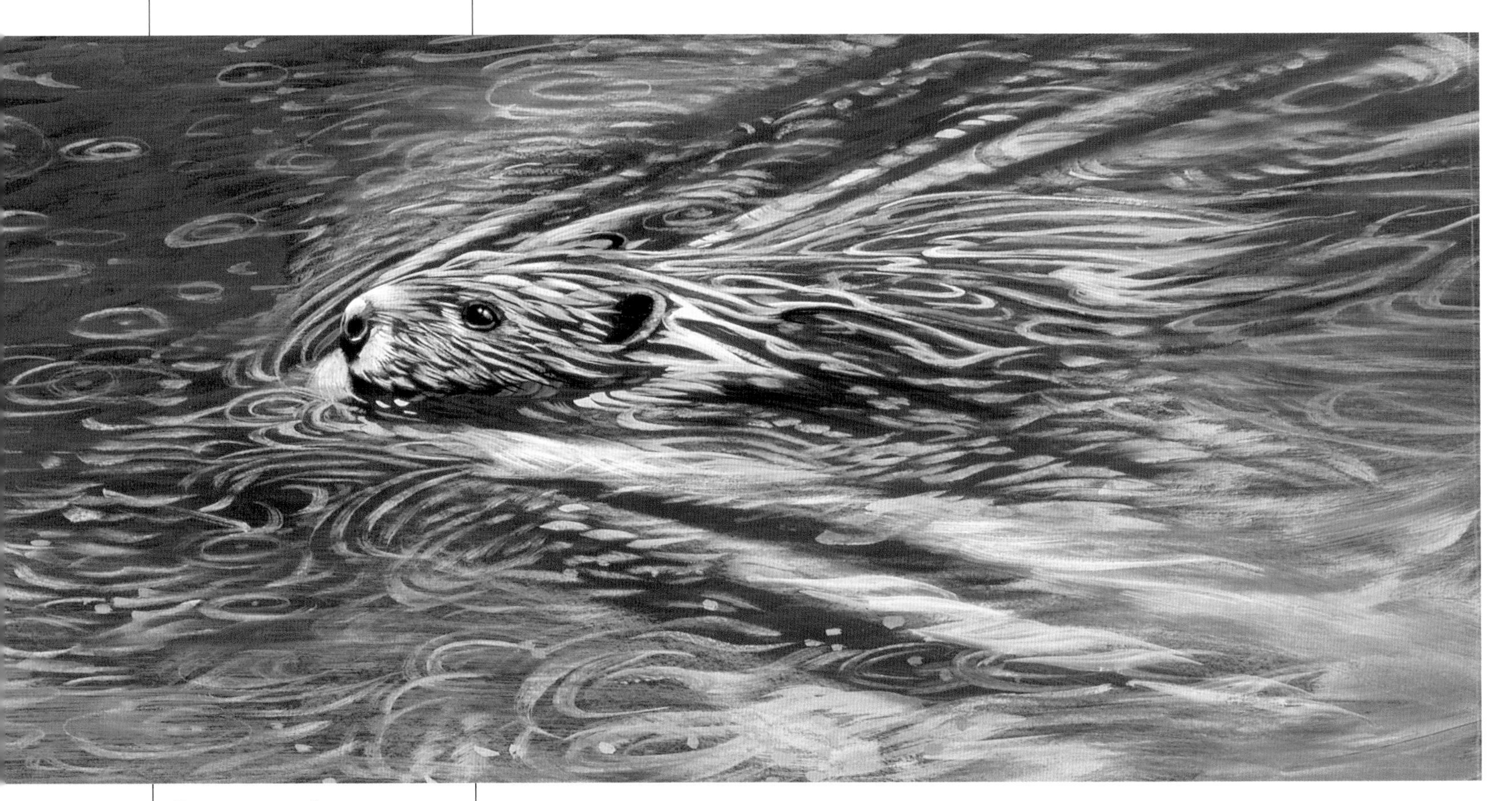

Swimming in the Rain
In the collection of Mr and Mrs Cooper

dummies sitting around polystyrene igloos will provide a gentle introduction to our forthcoming journey, we pay the museum a visit. I am in the process of bending down to have a closer look at a stuffed marmoset when I hear a distinctive ripping sound and realise to my acute embarrassment that the seat of my jeans has given way and split across the top of my thigh - probably in protest at the hearty breakfasts of pancakes and maple syrup I have been devouring in our hotels. I therefore spend the rest of the day enjoying the unique distinction of being the only visitor to the museum looking round with my back to the exhibits.

AN IMPRESSIVE WALL OF BRANCHES STUFFED WITH LEAVES AND MUD.

EAGER BEAVER

*Chapter Three*

# Hell Frozen Over

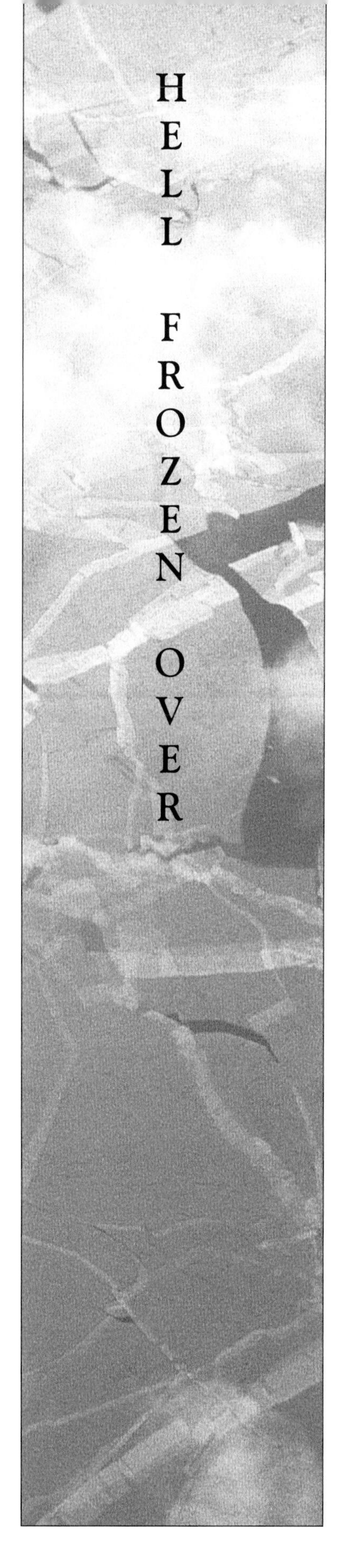

OUR arrival at the airport in Ottawa marks the start of our journey proper. We board a small aircraft, destination Iqualuit. Positioned on the southern tip of Baffin Island, the largest island in Canada, Iqualuit is the most northerly town of any significant size in this region. Chatting to a fellow passenger, an employee of the tiny television station IBC (The Inuit Broadcasting Corporation), I learn that most of the Canadian workers based here refer to it as 'Hell Frozen Over'. The majority of these workers are employed in the mining industry, which is the basis of the economy in the Northwest Territories. Fur trapping, fishing and the sale of native handcrafts contribute to a lesser degree.

Our overnight stop in a hotel close to the airport does not allow us much time to explore the delights conjured up by this affectionate nickname. We arrive late afternoon and decide to brave a stroll down the main street of town. During the day the snow covering the street has been turned into slush by the pedestrian traffic, but as the temperatures fall and the residents retreat indoors, a thin layer of ice is forming over the top, so clutching at each other for balance we slither and slide from building to building. Pollyanna steps on to a patch of ice which rather than concealing an inch of slush gives way to plunge her right leg into a foot deep puddle of icy water. The ensuing banshee-like shrieks send the rest of the town's occupants scurrying for cover, and us rapidly sliding our way back to the hotel to search out fresh, dry thermal socks.

Although we were able to buy most of the thermal and waterproof clothing required for our expedition in outdoor activity shops back home in the United Kingdom, we have taken advantage of our drive through Canada to purchase a couple of more specialist items. Firstly, we are now both the proud owners of a pair of double skin waterproof sorrel boots. These are several sizes too large to allow for additional pairs of socks and extend so far beyond the normal size and shape of my feet that I am prone to falling over invisible objects while wearing them. No doubt I will master the art of walking in sorrels over the coming weeks. The other

purchase is a huge, heavy-duty, down-filled purple jacket. This piece of clothing is nearly as big as I am. It is impossible to fold and resists all attempts at being crushed into a suitcase. I hang it in the hotel wardrobe. The wardrobe is full.

That evening we decide to visit the hotel restaurant for a final meal in civilisation before braving the rigours of outdoor catering. We are shown to a lovely table in the corner. Pollyanna shivers. The air conditioning is turned a little high. She is in a draught. She is cold. Can we move tables? This bodes well for the coming two weeks camping out on the ice floes.

IQUALUIT AIRPORT.

We arrive at the airport the following morning in good time and check as much luggage as possible into the hold, leaving us carrying a mere four bags and our down-filled jackets, which now appear to have taken on a life of their own, including distinct preferences for where they want to sit.

We depart from Iqualuit in a tiny Hawker Siddley aircraft. All our fellow passengers appear to be well over six feet tall and dressed in hairy jackets, with hairy faces to match. There is a female flight attendant on board and she is flying in the face of fashion by not sporting facial hair; but rather than the usual airline uniform of a smart suit and court shoes she is wearing a heavy boiler suit and thick padded moon boots. She does, however, serve an in-flight breakfast - a very large steak, two poached eggs, toast, cheese and biscuits, a raspberry cream bun, orange juice and coffee! Under normal circumstances this would see me through to coffee time, but sadly my appetite is not all it might be.

WE DEPART FROM IQUALUIT IN A TINY AIRCRAFT.

The seats on this little plane are unreserved and, as we are the last two passengers to embark, we cannot find two seats together. My new travelling companion is an aged Inuit who has been south to Iqualuit for medical treatment. He is dressed in his traditional clothing of furs from head to toe. As we are to discover later on, when the Inuit use animal skins for clothing they are not fully cured, in order to keep out the intense cold. In temperatures of –40°C the furs do not smell. In the warmer environment of an aircraft cabin, however, they give off a powerfully distinctive odour reminiscent of a dead fish left on a sunny windowsill for a week. This is a remarkably effective appetite suppressant.

Pollyanna visits the restroom facilities at the back of the tiny plane. She returns looking

pale and pauses at my seat, braving the spreading aura of putrefying trout, to pass on a piece of advice. If I need to visit the loo (and only if I really must) then I am to take care not to get disorientated. Whilst availing herself of the facilities she felt a chilly draught and looking to the side, realised that she was right next to the emergency exit door. This means that the door to the left leads back into the cabin, while the door to the right leads to instant death, sucked out of an aircraft into sub-zero temperatures.

As we fly north, the landscape spread out below the plane is gradually changing. The dark waters of the Arctic ocean are giving way to solid blocks of ice, until everything below us is white in every direction. It is impossible to tell where the land ends and the sea begins.

Eventually, the expanse is broken by a dark cluster of buildings, picked out clearly against the snow. This is our first sight of Igloolik, a small community on a tiny limestone island eight kilometres off the Canadian mainland, located 483 km north of the Arctic Circle. The Inuit name Igloolik literally translates as 'place of houses'. I peer eagerly down as the plane begins its descent. One thing I cannot make out is the runway. The reason for this soon becomes clear. There is no runway, just a smooth sheet of white ice on which our pilot skilfully lands the aircraft. Once safely down, I wrestle my jacket into submission and prepare to leave the plane.

As soon as I have negotiated the steps from the plane, and am standing on solid ground once again (or at least solid ice), I attempt to don the jacket. The pilot has advised us that the current temperature is –25°C and a fierce crosswind is blowing the snow into my face and whipping my hair across my vision. Pausing in my futile struggle, I realise the airport building is a mere eighteen metres away and I am unlikely to freeze to death walking to it, even without the protection of my jacket.

Igloolik International Airport consists of a small shed. As the door is opened to allow the newly arrived passengers in, a small snowdrift blows across the floor. A wooden table, which no doubt serves as the check-in desk for all destinations, is currently unoccupied. A couple of Inuit men unload the cases, trunks and crates of provisions from the hold. Our bags sit out on the runway gathering a layer of snow. Our friends at Canada North Outfitting inc. have assured us that on our arrival they would arrange for us to be met by an English-speaking

Igloolik International Airport consists of a small shed.

Information posters, one in Inuit script, the other a helpful English translation.

contact. We asked how we would recognise this person - would they carry a sign? Or should I wear a carnation and carry a copy of *The Times?* In reality it is quite clear that anyone who is expecting us will have no trouble at all in identifying us - for a start we are the only women to arrive on the flight. However, nobody rushes up to claim us. We sit down on a small plastic bench inside the airport building to wait. Gradually the airport empties, as the other passengers make their way into the town. We wait. A short while later we hear the sound of the plane flying back out, on its way to another remote community with the two remaining passengers and more crates of provisions flown up from the south. It is too late to back out now. Still we wait. The only entertainment to distract us is the information posters pinned to the wall, one in Inuit script, the other a helpful English translation.

Clearly aerial caribou buzzing is a regular problem in this part of the world. The Inuit script is fascinating - very graphic, composed of circles of various sizes, triangles, dots and lines. Apparently, the language is very complex, and hard for Europeans to learn; the basic grammatical construction being quite different from anything with which we are familiar. We do hope that we will be able to master one or two phrases during our visit. At the moment we could do with 'excuse me, we have just arrived from England and our contact isn't here to meet us, could you point me in the right direction?' but as the airport is now completely empty our lack of linguistic ability is fairly irrelevant.

Suddenly the door is thrust open and an Inuit gentleman bursts in, brushing the snow off his fur jacket. He grasps Pollyanna firmly by the hand and introduces himself as Luccassee. He apologises profusely for the delay in meeting us, but he had a little difficulty in finding the driver of the local taxi that will transport us to the boarding house where we will be staying overnight. All is now well and our transport awaits.

I step outside, but cannot see a taxicab. Or any car at all. This is the second time during this journey that I have had trouble identifying a vehicle and the first one turned out to be right beside me. I pause and look round carefully to avoid making a fool of myself in the first five minutes of meeting. Meanwhile Luccassee is cheerfully heaving our bags on to a wooden sledge and securing them with lengths of twine. A strong rope leads from the front of the sledge; following the length of it my eye comes to

The Inuit Bible.

rest on a skidoo. This is the taxi. The driver can only take one of us at a time, so I wait at the airport, while Pollyanna is ferried to the boarding house, and the driver then duly returns to collect me. Luccassee makes his way there on his own smaller skidoo.

The taxi.

Our drive takes us down the main street of Igloolik. A tiny community of one thousand people, Igloolik is the third largest settlement in the Baffin Island region. The Arctic Northwest Territories cover over a third of Canada's total area, but are home to less than 0.2% of the population, a mere fifty thousand people. The residents are subject to the same laws governing the rest of the country, despite their very different living conditions - including the compulsory education of all children under sixteen. Igloolik, like many of the communities in the territories, was established largely to accommodate this need by gathering the children together in one place. Prior to this, for the past four thousand years, the majority of the Iglulingmui, as the Inuit in this region are called, had led a nomadic existence, travelling in family groups over the ice, following the migrations of the animals on which they depended for food. Since our visit, the historical Nunavut agreement has given land and a greater autonomy to the Inuit people.

Catholics and Anglicans ventured into the frozen north to save souls.

Most of the single-storey wooden buildings look like they have been sent up in kit form, then hastily assembled. Snow is piled high on the corrugated iron roofs. We pass the Co-op store; seemingly the only shop in town, it also houses a coffee bar, the social centre of the community. The Co-op stocks canned goods, cereals, breads and some vegetables, flown up from the south. The foodstuffs are highly priced, due to the expense of importing them into the Arctic. It is not surprising that traditional hunting methods still provide over three quarters of the Inuit diet. There are two churches in this small community, built by the missionaries who arrived in the early 1900s. Both the Catholics and Anglicans ventured into the frozen north to save the souls of the heathens and both built their own houses of worship. Nearly one hundred years later the town is more or less split in two, with the Catholics living in the north side of the town near their church, the Anglicans on the south near their place of worship.

Behind the town, dominating the view, loom two huge cylindrical storage tanks, which hold the supply of oil for heating the houses. Outside most of the homes we pass there is a wooden framework with the skin of an animal stretched out to cure in the cold air. I recognise caribou

Anna-Louise in Igloolik.

fur, several sealskins, and on one huge frame the skin of a polar bear. I have flown 4,260km to see one and the first one I find is empty.

When I arrive at our accommodation, Pollyanna is already comfortably ensconced in an armchair, clutching a coffee, discussing our forthcoming expedition with Luccassee. He has arranged for two Inuit to guide us. Both men still provide for their families by hunting in the traditional way on the ice. They speak some English and are prepared to take us out by dog sled for twelve days. Between them they have identified the area they feel the polar bears are most likely to be found at this time of the year.

Room without a view!

Luccassee then leaves us to settle in, promising to return later. The boarding house we are staying in overnight primarily provides accommodation for the workers from the oil fields. They are mainly French Canadian and at the moment the only signs of their presence are French newspapers and the stubble left in the wash basin in the communal bathroom. A native of Igloolik runs the boarding house. On our arrival she is in the kitchen preparing the evening meal - seal stew. The Inuit women use a flat circular blade called an *ulu* to scrape away every bit of flesh from the skin, which will then be stretched out on a frame to cure.

When the preparations for the meal are well in hand our hostess settles down on a sofa to watch daytime television, freshly beamed up from the United States and southern Canada. The boarding house is heated inside to a subtropical 80 degrees Farenheit. During our stay we never see the owner step outside the door. Food is delivered to her doorstep and she walks round in a T-shirt, seemingly oblivious to the blizzard conditions outside her four walls. On the television screen, the hysterically dramatic plot lines of daytime soaps are interspersed with adverts for lawn mowers and sprinklers. 'Now it is springtime we need to turn our attention to cutting the grass and sharpening those rusty blades' intones a deep American accent, while a thick carpet of snow covers the street outside the window.

An appropriately shaped numberplate.

Asleep beside her on the sofa is our landlady's eighteen-month-old son, who rejoices in the seemingly unlikely name of Trevor. (For all I know this is also a traditional Inuit word meaning 'He who kills polar bears with his bare hands'.) The noise of the lawnmowers whirring across manicured lawns wakes him and he blinks sleepily at me. At home I can terrify small children simply by smiling benignly at them and when travelling in more remote places I am used to the sight of them running away, screaming in fear at the sight of my alien features. But instead of hiding behind the sofa, or cowering behind his mother's legs in floods of tears, Trevor beams back at me and holds out his chubby arms out to be picked up. This is new territory. Gingerly I lift him. Still no tears, until I try to put him down again a little while later. Trevor has formed an instant attachment. He is smitten. At any attempt to hand him back to his mother, or put him down on the sofa, his face creases up and the tears start. Thus I spend the rest of the day with a small Eskimo attached to my person, either sitting on my knee, or balanced on my hip as I walk.

Around 5.00 pm the construction workers return from their shift in the oil fields. As they step into the sauna-like atmosphere they are already divesting themselves of their layers of outside clothing, and by the time they reach the table they are dressed only in a motley assortment of vests, T-shirts and shorts. Although just six men are currently in residence the volume of conversation, a mixture of English and Canadian French, makes it sound as though we are dining with a twenty-strong delegation from the United Nations.

The vast cauldron of stew, which has been bubbling away on the stove, is set in front of us and rapidly devoured. Clearly the cold air has given the workers an appetite, as well as wind-burnt faces and reddened and chapped lips. Great interest is shown in our proposed journey into the vast wilderness and immediately bets are taken on how long we will survive before we beg our guides to return us to civilisation. The highest estimate is three nights. Their faith in us is touching.

After the meal, Luccassee returns, and we lay out all our carefully accumulated collection of clothing for him to inspect and approve. My unpacking is somewhat hampered by Trevor who is still clinging limpet-like to my side. Luccassee expertly fingers the fabrics, nodding at our fleeces, and tutting at one or two substandard items of thermal underwear designed for a chilly November day in Derbyshire. The down jackets meet with his approval, but when he reaches our precious sorrel boots he laughs. I am highly offended. These boots were not inexpensive, they are Canadian not English, and I am only just mastering the art of walking in them, surely they will keep me warm and dry? Luccassee shakes his head sorrowfully, but promises that

Preparing the evening meal.

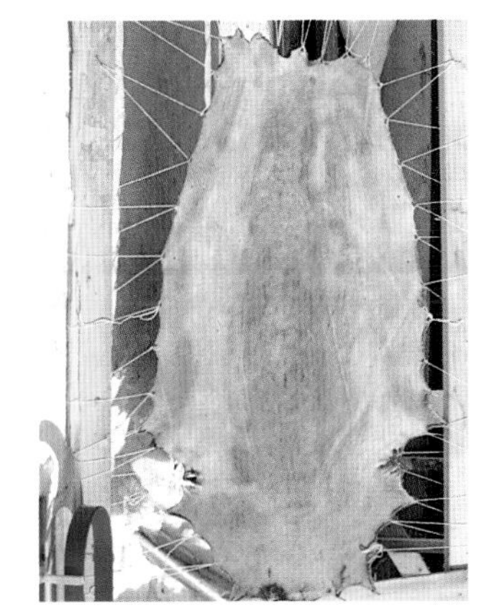

The skins of animals stretched out to cure.

And the first polar bear we see is empty.

Trevor samples Anna-Louise's Sunglasses.

when he returns in the morning he will try to provide some borrowed boots that will be more satisfactory.

He asks if we would like to take the opportunity to have a walk around Igloolik. We are pretty tired, but realise this will probably be our only chance to see the town. I finally detach a now sleepy Trevor, we pile on some extra layers of clothing and set out. One building is conspicuous among the low square houses of the community. The Igloolik research station stands like a concrete mushroom on the outskirts of the town, a circular raised building it has the appearance of a flying saucer about to take off. Luccassee leads us in and introduces us to John MacDonald, a Scot who has lived in Igloolik for seven years – and loves it. I ask him how he copes with the long dark days of winter, when the sun does not rise above the horizon for two months. He confides that he indulges in his favourite pastime, cross-country skiing. In the dark? At –60°C? These Scots are made of stern stuff. Clearly he is immune to the condition, which the Inuit call *perlerorneq* 'the weight of life', bought on by the long dark winter months.

John explains that the centre, with its modern laboratories, is used as the base for a wide variety of research - seismic, meteorological, cultural and biological. He is currently recording data about the weather, and a group of Canadian students is studying the interaction and play patterns of the Inuit children. Apparently their findings so far indicate that Inuit children do not smile as frequently as children from other cultures - they will not smile as a greeting for example. Taking an unqualified guess, I wonder if this has anything to do with the aforementioned *perlerorneq*.

Igloolik Research Station

Heading back into the main street of Igloolik, Luccassee leads us to one of the houses. He would like to introduce us to one of his friends, Sam. Sam is an Inuit hunter who still uses many of the traditional methods to catch his quarry. He welcomes us into his home. We step straight into the sparsely furnished main room and perch on the edge of one of two sofas. A shelving unit stands against the wall opposite, but bizarrely it is almost empty, with a scattering of books, boxes and assorted objects on the floor at the base. Luccassee asks if we would be interested in learning more about the Inuit methods of hunting and we nod politely. A short discussion ensues and Sam fetches an array of objects from a side room. The first item held out for our inspection appears to be a whole empty sealskin with a tube at one end. Sam explains that it is a whole empty sealskin with a tube at one end. This is a float used to track the harpooned animal when spearing narwhals and walruses. Sam demonstrates how it can be flattened and then re-inflated by blowing into the tube, which is grotesquely stuck where the mouth used to be. He flattens and inflates, flattens and inflates, bounces the seal like a football, flattens and inflates. I am starting to feel a little queasy. He asks if I would like a go, proffering the tube with great enthusiasm, I decline. I am starting to worry that I may faint - the house is warm and I am still wearing my outside layers. The skins are not fully cured and I am more used to signing petitions to save seals rather than inflating their empty skins. Out here hunting is not a sport, it is survival. Like any predators the Inuit have to live in balance with their prey. In days gone by if the animals were over hunted their numbers would decline and the people would starve and die until the balance was redressed.

Sam moves on to show us an array of spears and harpoons made from the bones of various animals. In this civilisation, which is totally reliant on hunting for food, no part of the animal is wasted. Skins are made into clothing, storage bags and shoes. The bones are made into spears, tools and sewing needles. He shows us toys which he has crafted from bones for his children: a spinning and whistling toy made from the carved bone of a wolf's foot looped on to a leather thong, and a catching game created from a spinal vertebrae attached to a thin bone by a fine strap. From the tiny bones of a fox's foot he has made a minute sledge and husky dog team, complete with a little leather harness, which is quite enchanting.

Seeing that we are impressed, he warms to his theme and brings out his personal collection of 'interesting bones'. We are treated to a walrus tusk, surprisingly large and heavy, the thigh bone from the largest caribou he has ever trapped and a narwhal penis bone, easily three feet long. He graphically demonstrates which part of the narwhal's anatomy the bone came from in case we are having trouble following. We smile and nod, somewhat at a loss for words while trying to look suitably impressed. It obviously works because Sam offers us the bone as a gift. We decline politely, explaining that it would not be possible for us to take it back through customs, although we are touched by his generosity.

A selection of animal pelts follows, including sealskin in various stages - dried out and hard

Skins are made into clothing, storage bags and shoes.

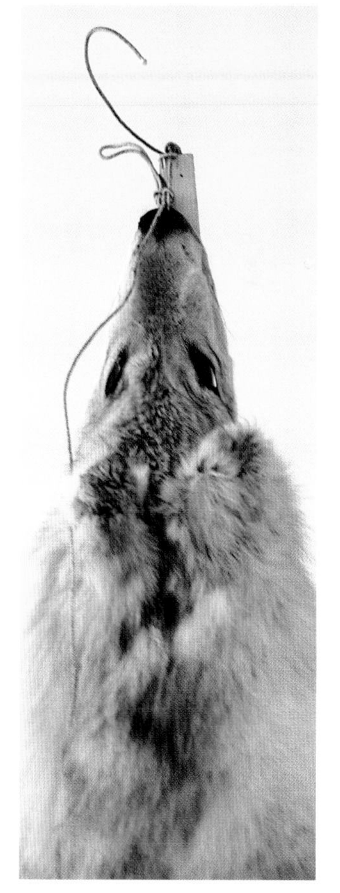

Wolf skin drying.

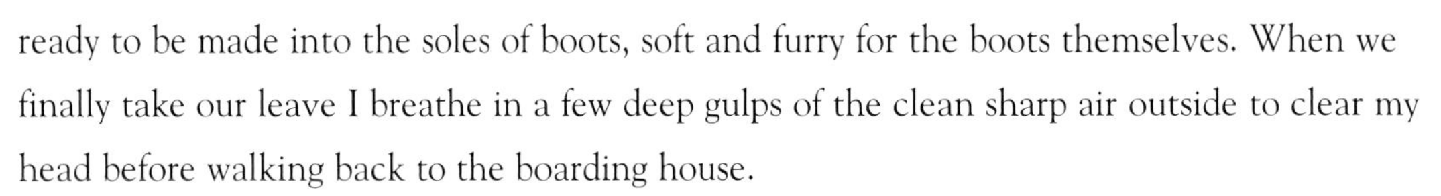

ready to be made into the soles of boots, soft and furry for the boots themselves. When we finally take our leave I breathe in a few deep gulps of the clean sharp air outside to clear my head before walking back to the boarding house.

We retire to our bedroom and try to reorganise our packing so that we can take just the bare essentials and leave our large cases in the boarding house until our return - there is a limit to the amount we can take out on the dog sleds. Fortunately, we will be wearing all of our clothing in one go, thus creating some space in our bags. I am reluctant to leave the warmth of the boarding house for the wilderness, but Pollyanna is convinced the only way to experience this environment is to travel through the Arctic living as the Inuit live upon the ice. She is able to reduce the quantity of art materials she will be carrying - evidently in these temperatures her watercolours will be useless. If we are lucky enough to find any wildlife she will have to sketch using lead pencils. I sort through my toiletries (moist wipes - essential, lipstick - guess not) and in the process suffer my first major panic attack. Until now I have been able to concentrate on the organisation, the packing, the timetable, but now I am faced with the reality of heading out into the Arctic. With a tent. What could I have been thinking of? Do I look like Ranulph Feinnes? Why didn't Pollyanna decide to paint for an exhibition of exotic seashells or small tropical fish?

Packing complete, I barricade myself in the bathroom, only too horribly aware that this is the last occasion I will have access to running water for some time. I intend to make the most of it. For some unaccountable reason Pollyanna seems to find the sight of me sitting on the end of the bed drying and styling my hair, and applying nail varnish, highly amusing.

Northern Exposure

*Have you ever heard of the Land of Beyond?*
*That dreams at the gates of the day?*
*Alluring it lies at the skirts of the skies*
*And ever so far away.*

ROBERT SERVICE
YUKON POET

## DAY ONE (MORNING): I MAY BE GONE SOMETIME

WE wake to a morning that is bright and clear, but extremely cold. It has snowed in the night and north winds have blown a thick drift of snow against our window, so we blearily peer at a view of white blankness. The condemned women join the construction workers to eat a hearty breakfast. They inform us that the weather is unusually cold for the Arctic spring - the thermometer outside is registering –30°C, the usual for this time of year would be ten degrees higher. Our landlady asks if we slept well and we assure her that we were very comfortable - although we were woken a couple of times by the sound of children playing in the street in the early hours of the morning. Apparently, we are told, this is not uncommon. The Inuit tend to have large families (Luccassee tells us later he has fourteen brothers and sisters) and there is often not enough room in the small houses for all the children to sleep in comfort. So in spring and summer, when the nights are light, the children sleep in shifts, one group curled up in bed, while their siblings play outside.

Before the advent of regular medical services, infant and child mortality rates were high. In this region, as in many areas of the Arctic, it is not uncommon for mothers to hand newborn children to relatives and friends to be raised. If a neighbour has just two children and you give birth to an eighth, it would be common practice to send the baby next door to be reared. To our European eyes this seems a very haphazard system of child rearing, but it is a custom that dates back centuries, and a practice that has not been eradicated by modern Canadian bureaucracy.

Luccassee arrives bright and early to assist us in our final preparations for departure. He is carrying additional clothing, which he has begged and borrowed from friends. We are now

each the proud (temporary) owners of a pair of thick socks, made from thick caribou felt. My socks are bright blue, while Pollyanna's are a soft creamy white with a pattern of brightly coloured birds in flight running around the tops of her calves. Luccassee informs us that they are men's socks, identifiable by the fact that the stitch work runs horizontally around the top. For women, the patterns would run down the leg of the sock, but as we are taller than most Inuit women, we have correspondingly larger feet. I am sure the polar bears won't laugh at our cross-dressing. The style and design of the socks traditionally represent the age, sex and place of origin of the wearer and often include images of animals. Also borrowed from Luccassee's male friends are two very impressive pairs of boots. The soles and uppers are sealskin, stitched together with a heavy thread, topped with thick fur to the knee. As keen conservationists, neither Pollyanna nor myself owns or wears furs back home in England. The Arctic, however, is an environment unlike any other to be inhabited by mankind and the usual rules and choices do not always apply. Man has not yet invented any material which will protect from the biting cold of this atmosphere as thoroughly as skins, so clothing here is made in the same way as it has been for centuries, from the partially cured hides of animals. If the skins were cured completely, as they would be back home, they would begin to let the cold through and be less effective. Out of curiosity, Pollyanna asks Luccassee how much it would cost to buy a pair of boots like the ones she is wearing. Luccassee quotes a price in Canadian dollars, but then casting a sly glance out of the corner of his eye, informs us that the boots would cost less if we chewed our own sealskin.

Apparently, when the skins have been hanging outside they become rigid and in order to make them soft enough to sew, the Inuit women sit and chew them until they are pliable. It is in fact this chewing, rather than any part of their diet, which accounts for the blackened teeth often seen in *National Geographic* photos of Inuits.

I AM SPHERICAL.

Once I have laced the front of the boots, my survival outfit is complete. By the time we step out of the door, I am wearing the following:

1 *Thermal silk vest*
2 *Thin, thermal silk tights*
3 *Thermal wool vest*
4 *Thermal leggings*
5 *Another pair of thermal leggings*
6 *Fleece sweater*
7 *Fleece jacket*
8 *Fleece leggings*
9 *Padded trousers*
10 *Waterproof over-trousers*
11 *Thermal socks*
12 *Another pair of thermal socks*
13 *Woollen socks*
14 *Felt socks*
15 *Sealskin boots*
16 *Fine silk thermal gloves*
17 *Fleece mittens*
18 *Padded ski mittens*
19 *Facemask*
20 *Goggles*
21 *Ski hat*
22 *The purple down jacket. With the hood up*

Homage a Kiraz

I am spherical.

My arms are sticking out practically at right angles. My movements are severely hampered. And apparently this is not sufficient. In the event that the weather should become any colder, Luccassee has also provided us with over jackets to wear on top of

THE OCEAN IS FROZEN TO A DEPTH OF 3 METRES.

the down jackets. Quite how I am supposed to pull a twenty-third item of clothing over my head is not readily apparent, and I fervently hope the temperatures will not drop.

Before leaving home, I discovered that the insulation value of cold weather clothing is measured in 'clo units'. Thus one of my smart business suits would have a rating of one clo (in layman's terms, laughably useless) while a traditional Inuit outfit made of seal and caribou skins notches up between eight and twelve clos (translation – you are warm, but rendered immobile with layers).

With some difficulty I hug Trevor goodbye and Luccassee leads us down to the edge of the town to meet our dog teams, and our human companions for our journey. Igloolik is built on the coast and we are to meet at the ocean's edge. For a brief ten weeks during summer, waves will lap at the shoreline and the townspeople will be able to use the few boats we see dotted about. Currently, however, the ocean is frozen to a depth of three metres and we will be travelling across it. In a sudden and unexpected change of anxieties, I find myself wondering what happens if we experience a sudden spell of unseasonably mild weather. Will the ice melt beneath us, plunging us into the dark depths, weighed down by wearing the entire contents of our suitcases at once?

I keep these thoughts to myself as Luccassee introduces us to our guides, Gideon and Pakka. Native Inuit, they live in Igloolik and both own a dog team. Gideon runs eleven huskies and Pakka a slightly smaller team of nine. When we arrive they are already loading provisions and tools into large crates on the back of the long wooden sleds. Food, camping stoves, fuel, candles, saws and sharp knives are all packed tightly in and the lid secured. Rifles are fixed on the top - for our protection in the event of a bear attack. Our bags are strapped in front of the boxes, and canvas bags holding the tents lashed on top of these. My bedding rolls are strapped on and finally blankets and furs are spread on the front part of each sled to give us a comfortable place to sit.

On the very back of the sledge, Gideon straps a huge chunk of frozen caribou meat. The Arctic acts as a huge natural freezer in which to preserve food, so this meat will last throughout our journey. Behind the crate on his sled, Pakka ties two huge seals, still whole, but again frozen solid. Averting my eyes from this sight, I unpack a camera to record our departure. This involves removing my top glove, which I do with some trepidation, convinced that frostbite will strike instantly through the remaining two layers.

News of the two English women who are going out on the ice to look for bears has spread rapidly through the community and a surprisingly large crowd is in attendance to see us off. Children run round our sleds, gazing up at us with huge solemn eyes, while the adults stand in groups, pointing and calling out, commenting mainly I imagine, on my shape in the twenty-two items of clothing. More acclimatised to the freezing conditions, the Inuit, although warmly dressed, are able to dispense with one or two layers of thermals and thus remain vaguely human in outline.

Eventually Luccassee approaches. The preparations are complete. Everything is in order, the dogs are ready. If something is not loaded into the sleds now, we will have to manage without it. He gravely shakes our hands and by way of a final pep talk instructs us on the actions to take in the event of a polar bear attack. We are instructed to make a lot of noise, stand our ground and 'act dominant' (sic). If we show signs of weakness, or try to run, the bear is more likely to attack. If we stand and face a charging bear head on, it will, in theory, back off. It is the 'in theory' part of the instructions that is bothering me. Has anyone put this advice to the test and lived to tell the tale? If the worst comes to the worst he continues, and the bear gets hold of me, play dead. I feel this may be all too easy. Luccassee looks confident enough - smiling broadly he wishes us a safe journey and many polar bears.

I clamber on to the sled and make myself comfortable on the bundles of blankets and furs. Pakka will sit in front of me and steer the dogs. Pollyanna will travel behind Gideon on the other sled. Pakka approaches, shaking his head. I am not sitting correctly. He motions for me to turn until I am sitting in a 'side-saddle' position. Luccassee hurries over to explain that it is better to sit sideways on a sled, so that the cold winds will not blow into my face when I travel.

Pollyanna settles on to her sledge which is slightly longer than the one I am travelling on. Gideon completes his last checks on the harnesses of his

dog team, climbs aboard, and suddenly they are moving. Pakka hops nimbly on to our sled in front of me and the huskies immediately leap up and start to pull forward. The assembled townspeople wave and call out to us as we depart, despite the fact that they no doubt expect to see our sleds returning within the day. We move slowly, the snow crunching under the runners, gathering momentum as the dogs gather speed.

We are off.

Above and Below: The sleds are packed with tools, food and provisions to cover any eventuality. Furs and blankets offer a comfortable seat at the front.

We follow the tracks made by Pollyanna's sled, already a small shape way ahead of us. I am taken aback by this, I had imagined that we would travel along side-by-side, able to chat casually as we made our way along. Behind us, Igloolik slowly recedes and in a surprisingly short time the town, and with it the last vestiges of civilisation, is out of sight. All around the world is white. For the first time since flying north, I have a taste of the true vastness of the ice-stilled landscape of the High Arctic. Without a familiar object to focus on - a building, a tree, even a rock - it is hard to judge distances, or to get any sense of the scale of the landscape in front of me. I can see the curving horizon line, an unbroken circle in front and behind. Distances in the Arctic are deceptive. The lack of dust in the atmosphere makes it possible to see for tens of miles across the fields of ice - and the lack of landmarks makes it impossible to tell if you are looking over one or one hundred miles of featureless white. The impression is truly of riding across the top of the world, where the air is still crisp and clean, of moving over the white arc at the top of the globe, the rest of the world falling away beneath us.

Away from the buildings I feel for the first time that we have reached the true Arctic. To a biologist, the Arctic is the region that occurs above the tree line. A climatologist would define the Arctic as a region with an average temperature of no more that 10°C during the warmest months of the year. To an oceanographer it coincides with the furthest reaches of the ever-shifting pack ice. I have come across many definitions during my research, but none has prepared me for the barren cold reality of such a vast untouched wilderness. Now I am here this land of extremes and contradictions seems almost to

defy definition - we are experiencing constant daylight, but for many weeks there will be constant darkness. It appears barren, but supports a myriad of life. Habitat is a vital part of every animal's existence. We are here because Pollyanna wanted to experience the Arctic of her imagination, so that when she paints the polar bear she can convey the unique relationship between animal and environment.

An eerie silence falls across the world, the only sounds the squeaking of the sledge runners on the snow and the panting of the husky team. As we travel on the very first stage of our journey, I am constantly making a mental count of my toes, wiggling them inside the layers of socks and boots, to check that there is still circulation and movement. Having been given so many dire warnings about the dangers of frostbite, I am convinced that within minutes of departure the ends of my fingers will turn black and drop off. When we have been travelling for half an hour, a part of my mind is quite surprised to find I am still in possession of a full set of digits. Encouraged by this, and wanting to adjust my goggles, I gingerly remove all four layers of gloves from my right hand. All is well, and I am starting to think that the dangers

have been hugely exaggerated, when I touch the front of my goggles. The sensation on touching the icy surface is not so much of cold, but rather of pain - rather like touching the surface of a radiator, which is so hot that on first contact it feels cold. The iciness of the air is also starting to register and my hand feels like it is starting to shrivel and wither. I hastily stick two layers of gloves back on and fumble with the goggles through the fabric.

In removing my gloves, I have learnt my first lesson about exposing my skin. As little as possible, as rapidly as possible. I am also learning very quickly that equipment purchased with confidence back in the United Kingdom will not always behave as hoped and imagined when put to the test in the Arctic. My tinted goggles, vital to protect my eyes not only from the intense, unremitting brightness of the snow, but also the bitter cold, were chosen to be worn in conjunction with a face mask. The mask, made from a warm fleece (in a particularly intense shade of green), fits over my head like a balaclava, but rather than having holes cut out for the eyes and mouth, it is split half-way down. The split ensures that the forehead is always covered, while the bottom half of the mask can be adjusted from below the chin to above the nose - very useful when wanting to eat and drink. I had intended to wear the mask over my nose, tucked under the bottom edge of the goggles, and initially this seems ideal, keeping my face entirely warm. The drawback, however, is that if I decide to indulge in the luxury of breathing the mask directs my out-breath up inside the goggles; the warm air meets the cold surface of the Perspex and condenses on contact. Seconds later the condensation freezes, leaving me peering out at the Arctic through a cloudy layer of ice. When I remove my goggles to scrape out the ice, the moisture on my eyelashes instantly freezes as the cold air reaches my eyes. This is a major problem. If I want to see anything at all, I will have to either stop breathing, or wear the mask below my nose. When I try this, I can feel the inside of my nostrils freezing as I breathe the icy air. In the end I compromise, covering the very tip of my nose only, while covering the exposed skin with a liberal layer of lip balm, which

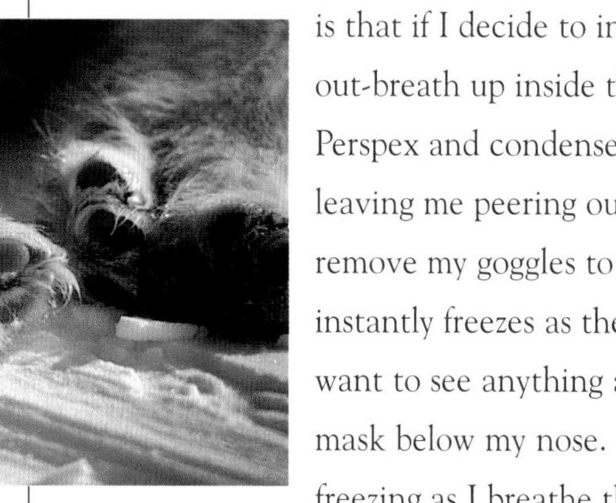

THE HUSKIES ROLL IN THE SNOW TO COOL DOWN.

contains a very high factor sun block, to protect myself from exposure to the sun, reflected back from the glaring whiteness of my surroundings.

Fortunately, Pollyanna is not having these problems - her knitted white mask is a more traditional balaclava style, and her goggles fit over the eye holes. The round hole for her mouth is outlined in vivid red stitching, removing the need for any lipstick, but giving her a permanent expression of mildly shocked surprise.

I am still fiddling with the mask and goggles when I realise that Pollyanna and Gideon have stopped a little way ahead on the ice and Pakka is now drawing our sled up to stop alongside them. There is much noise and excitement as our two husky teams greet each other. Pollyanna clambers off her sled and we rush to talk - congratulating ourselves on surviving this first tiny test, still exclaiming over the fact that we are travelling across the surface of an ocean. Pollyanna asks if I saw the raven that flew

overhead a little earlier and I have to explain that at the moment I am having difficulty seeing anything at all. Meanwhile, Gideon and Pakka are delving in the cargo boxes. Pakka removes a red camping stove, setting it down on the lid of the crate, which he has placed on the snow. He scoops up a handful of snow and places it in a large battered black kettle. Up here the snow is so pure and uncontaminated, it is quite safe to drink the melted water. He explains in halting English that we will make frequent stops for cups of tea and small snacks, partly because we need to eat frequently, partly so that we can stretch our legs after long periods of sitting still, but mostly to give the huskies a chance to rest. Although the dogs are extremely fit, and very used to working, pulling the sleds demands a lot of energy. As soon as we stop, the dogs roll in the deep snow to cool themselves down, then settle down to doze.

While Pakka is finding tea bags and enamel mugs, Gideon is hard at work a short distance away. He is cutting out large blocks of snow in order to build a low semi-circular wall, a sort of 'demi-igloo'. This process is remarkably swift. When the wall is three blocks of snow in height he rejoins us and, gesturing towards this construction, he announces in a voice filled with pride 'The Restroom!'. As he has gone to so much trouble, I feel obliged to use the facilities. Quickly. I am pleasantly surprised by this touch of civilisation - at least we have been provided with a little bit of privacy, as well as shelter from the worst of the winds. If Gideon builds us a ladies loo every time we stop, perhaps this will not be as bad as I feared. Within half an hour, we have packed our tea things away, secured the sledges, and are ready to move on. We are blissfully unaware that for the duration of our adventure Gideon and Pakka will never build another restroom.

*Somewhere out on the sea ice roams the majestic polar bear, the symbol of the Arctic, object of our quest. The polar bear is the largest, most dangerous and most respected Arctic land mammal. For many thousands of years the Inuit have feared him, hunted him and worshipped him. Polar bears are the largest members of the bear family. An adult male can weigh up to 590 kgs. They can grow to 3.4 m from nose to tail - though the largest recorded polar bear was over 3.7 m in length and weighed in at an impressive 1002 kgs. Despite this they are capable of running at speeds of 40 kmph for short bursts. Polar bears have a longer neck and smaller head than other bears. The massive forepaws, up to 30 cms in diameter, almost as broad as they are long, have partially webbed toes to help the bear to swim. The soles of the feet are covered in dense thick fur, helping to grip the ice and provide protection from the cold. They have an incredibly well developed sense of smell - the Alaskan Inuit claim that a bear can smell a whale carcass from 80 kms away. Back in 1594 Gerritt de Veerthe, chronicler of Barents voyages, observed that the bears 'smell farthre than they see'.*

Day One (Afternoon): Eaters of Raw Meat

The Arctic was first named by ancient astronomers observing Ursa Major (the great bear) and Ursa Minor (the little bear). They named the uncharted lands above which these constellations appeared *Arktikos* from the Greek word for bear. We are therefore travelling through the country of the bear both literally and figuratively. The first Arctic explorer was probably also Greek. Pytheas is believed to have sailed from his home as far as Iceland in 825 BC and ever since then legends and stories from this frozen white world have held a deep fascination for mankind.

Every block of ice, every drift of snow seems to be moving. Several times an hour I see the distinct shape of a polar bear, ambling across the frozen surface, white on white. But my brain is playing tricks on me. I am so keen to find a bear, I am imagining one in each snowdrift. In this first day's travelling the only other live creatures we have seen are the black silhouettes of ravens flying overhead, occasionally alighting briefly on the ice a little way from our sledges. The only black creature in a world of white, they stand out harshly, seeming out of place in the realm of the white bears, foxes, owls and seals. Pakka tells us that the Inuit have many legends about these black interlopers. In olden days, it was told that Raven stole the sunlight at the end of summer, plunging the Arctic into three long months of absolute darkness.

By mid-afternoon the weather is deteriorating. The skies are grey, the temperatures have dropped further and the winds are strengthening. Gideon feels that we could be in for a blizzard, and suggests we find a suitable place to pitch camp and batten down for the night. He is afraid that with the overcast sky we may experience 'whiteout', this is when it becomes impossible to see the horizon between the earth and sky, the most dangerous and disorientating travel conditions. Because the winds are so bad our guides fear that it will not be possible to put up the tents securely and decide, after some discussion, that it will be necessary for them to build igloos. Secretly Pollyanna and I are delighted. The search begins for suitable snow. The Inuit understandably have many words to describe different types of snow as it has such a huge influence over their lives. *Qanik*, for example, is fine-grained, powdered snow. *Sastugi* is hard snow fluted into dunes by the wind. *Mowya* is slushy wet snow, which sits on top of the ice and makes driving conditions difficult.

Building an igloo - a skill handed down over generations.

Not all snow is the right consistency for the construction of an igloo: too soft, the building will crumble; too hard, the blocks will crack as they are cut. Apparently, the ideal material is a layer of snow which has been formed from a single storm. Gideon moves from place to place testing the snow. Finally, the ideal area is found. Not accustomed to having to build our house before retiring to bed for the night, Pollyanna and I are reduced to sitting on the sledge, spectating as Gideon and Pakka set to work. Pollyanna sketches in short bursts, capturing the various stages of construction. Using a traditional snow knife called a *pannak*, Gideon draws a large circle freehand on the surface of the snow. From within the circle he starts to cut out rectangular blocks vertically from the snow. The resulting hollow will form the floor of our house. As he cuts, Pakka lifts the blocks out by the lower corners and starts construction, laying the first row of blocks side by side around the outside edge of the circle. With a skill handed down over generations, and evidently borne of long practice, he slices an angular piece of snow from the top of the blocks so that the second layer will start to slope inwards, and gradually the structure will curve towards a central point. Each new block of snow is carefully shaved to fit on top of the foundations, pushed into to place, and secured with a hard blow. Finally a circular 'roof' is lowered into place, the edges locking with the now sharply angled top of the final blocks. Pollyanna and I are finally given a job that we can be trusted to carry out without any previous experience - we carefully go round the igloo, pushing snow into any gaps and chinks between the blocks to seal any gaps remaining. Gideon uses further blocks to make two small walls leading up to the low arched doorway. He and Pakka then start laying furs inside the tents; these, along with our sleeping rolls, will form a soft and warm base for our sleeping bags. Finally, our bags are eased through the small opening, and our home is ready. Gideon and Pakka then set to work all over again, and repeat the whole process to build themselves a shelter for the night.

Construction work over, it is dinnertime. Gideon and Pakka declare themselves starving after their physical work, and I am quite peckish myself. We are aware that we need to eat a lot more than usual in this environment - we have been advised to take in between four thousand and five thousand calories a day in order to compensate for the extra energy used in keeping warm, and to maintain our body weight.

Gideon and Pakka unpack plates, forks and mugs. We offer to help unload the cargo boxes, but our assistance does not seem to be welcome, and we are shooed away to sit down on the sledges until the food is prepared. Gideon produces a huge knife, the thick blade glinting as he walks to the back of the sled and cuts off a hunk of the frozen caribou meat. Kneeling down, he then uses the same knife to cut the meat into delicate slices, which he portions out on to four plates and hands round. Presumably we now have to cook our own dinner - but the method is not obvious. The kettle is on the stove - perhaps once the water has boiled we will cook the meat barbecue style over the flames? But Gideon and Pakka are already tucking in with relish. I look at them. I look at my plate. The slices of meat look back at me. Frozen. And raw. Back home in England, Pollyanna and I eat a predominently vegetarian diet. We had been well aware before setting out that we would have no choice but to eat meat on this expedition. In the High Arctic it is impossible to grow vegetables for much of the year and we knew we would not have the luxury of sitting on the back of the sledges and announcing 'I'll have the salad'. However, I had not bargained on my first taste of red meat in several years being raw. Nervously I take a bite. I am hoping that this will be one of those exotic delicacies, which sounds inedible but in reality is delicious. It is not. A solid block, the meat is ice cold, and flavourless. Watching Gideon and Pakka, we follow their example, and chew until the meat is soft enough to swallow. With grim determination I clear my plate, Gideon offers seconds. We both decline. In many parts of the Arctic it is considered insulting to use the word 'Eskimo'. This is a Native American word meaning 'eaters of raw meat' and is considered derogatory, a fact I reflect on as I am doggedly chewing. 'Inuit' is the preferred term, and means simply 'the people' in their own language.

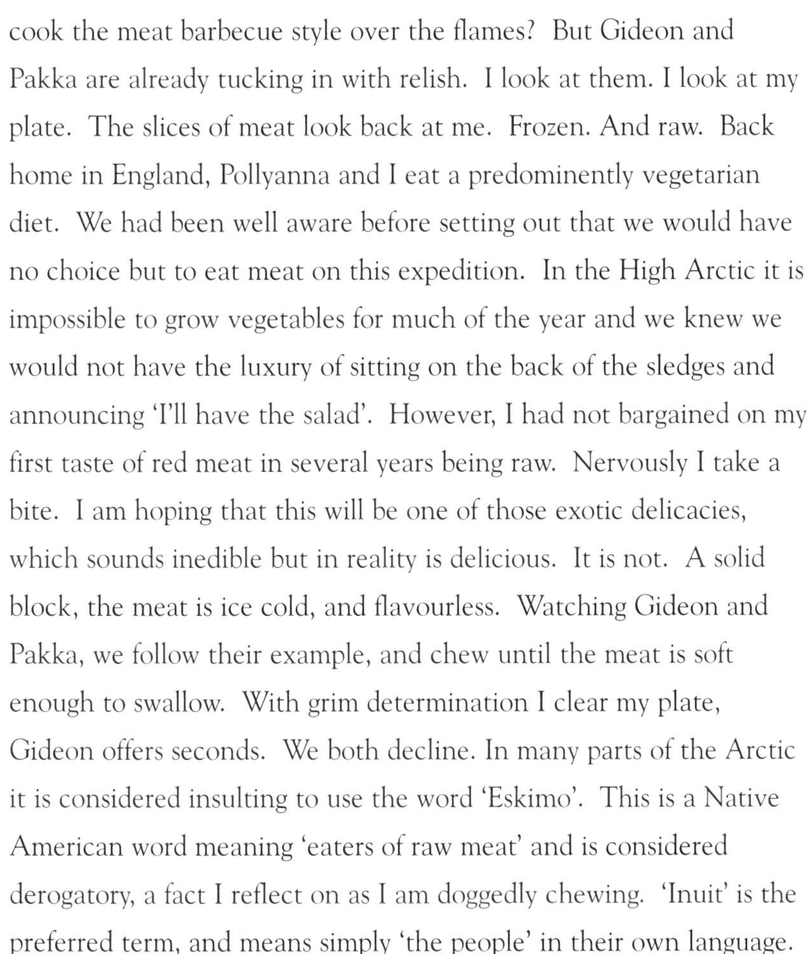

Arctic cookery.

Our first Arctic home.

The Arctic is not the area to choose a vegetarian diet. Little can grow in the permafrost. The Arctic topsoil is low in nutrients and the short, cool growing season sustains only very few perennial plants. The growth rate for these plants is so slow - some lichens take ten years to grow one inch out on the tundra - that typically they will not fruit and flower for the first time until several years after planting. The few naturally occurring grasses and lichens do, however, provide enough meagre rations to sustain many Arctic animals - including large herds of caribou that roam throughout the Arctic. The caribou themselves are the principal source of food for both humans and wolves. In fact, historically, 'vegetable' to many Inuit people would have indicated the contents of a caribou's stomach - a half digested, green, acidulous mass. This would be eaten either frozen alongside the meat, or boiled into a soup.

Gratefully, I drink the black tea and, with our meal over, it is time to bed down for the night. We are able to use the rest of the water that has been boiled for tea, and which is now rapidly cooling, to wash our hands and clean our teeth. I have brought along plentiful supplies of sealed wipes, but when I reach into the bag to retrieve one I realise that in these temperatures the liquid in the tissues has frozen solid. We slip several of the little packets into inner pockets, to encourage them to thaw out to body temperature so that we can use them in the morning. From the outside the igloo that Pollyanna and I are to share does not appear large enough for us to lie down inside, full length, in our sleeping bags. Appearances prove to be deceptive - Tardis-like the igloo provides us with ample space.

Pakka passes us a candle, to provide warmth. Lighting a stove in this confined space would generate too much heat (with obvious and very wet consequences). Due to the insulating properties of snow, a single candle can raise the temperature inside an igloo by 40°F. There is a round hole cut into the roof to allow the air to circulate and to prevent the candle from burning up all of our oxygen. Pakka cuts a large slab of snow, carefully curves the top and then blocks up the entrance so that we are completely sealed in. The gaps between the blocks will quickly ice over, and the cold winds will be unable to penetrate the walls.

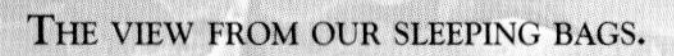

THE VIEW FROM OUR SLEEPING BAGS.

It occurs to me as the last block goes in that we are now completely isolated in this semi-circular cocoon. If Gideon and Pakka decided to leave us now we would not even be aware of their departure until morning, when we would awake to find ourselves stranded. So far we are only a day's journey from Igloolik, but we would have no idea how to start making our way back. Banishing these unnerving thoughts, I start to remove my boots, hampered considerably by the amount of clothing I am wearing - I can barely reach my feet. Some time later my boots are standing by my canvas bag. And that's me changed and ready for bed. I realise that this is the only expedition I have ever been on, where I put on every item of clothing I have brought on the first day, and am unlikely to remove anything until the day I return.

*Like the Inuit, polar bears hunt to survive and live primarily on a diet of raw meat. Their diet is almost exclusively carnivorous and consists mainly of sea mammals – seals and walruses. The bears will also scavenge, eating carrion such as beached whales, fish and crabs. On average, a bear will hunt a seal every 5 or 6 days, but while out on the ice can go for weeks without eating, living off reserves of fat. Polar bears have a huge stomach and are capable of eating up to 68 kg of food in one sitting, thus taking full advantage of every kill. In the summertime, the thaw may force bears on to land and they roam the coast looking for food. At this time they will eat almost anything to maintain body weight - birds, rodents, eggs, reindeer, even occasionally berries and plants. The summer is essentially a time of weight loss when the bears are subsisting on stored fat from the winter's seal hunt.*

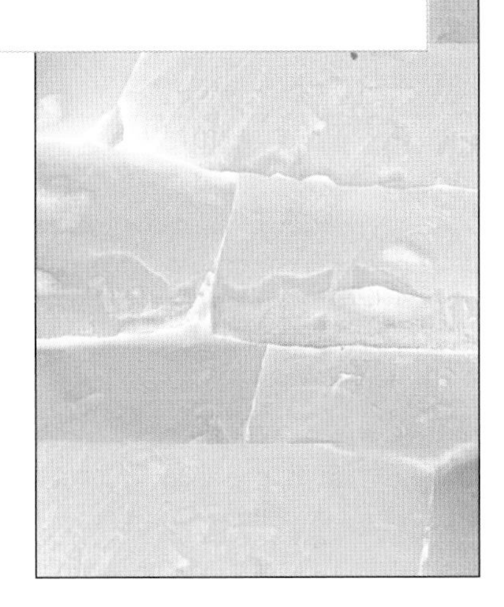

EMERGING AFTER A SURPRISINGLY GOOD NIGHT'S REST.

## DAY TWO (MORNING): THE LAND OF BEYOND

Against all the odds I have slept well, exhausted by the excitement of the first day. When I awake and crawl out of my sleeping bag, I find that Pollyanna is already up, has kicked out the entrance block of snow and is sitting outside the igloo, sketching the only animals we have seen so far - our husky team. Working in these temperatures presents her with a unique set of problems. Pollyanna is only able to sketch with pencils, all her other art materials are frozen solid. Because of the extreme cold, she cannot have her hands exposed to the air. As an artist, she has an even greater fear of frostbite than most Arctic explorers. Removing all but the thinnest layer of thermal gloves she can sketch in ten-minute bursts before her fingers start to feel numb, at which point she pulls the other two layers of gloves back on or lights one of the portable hand warmers we bought in Canada. These contain slow-burning strips of charcoal inside a metal case, which is then ensconced in a soft red cover - they give off a delightful and much needed warmth. We have found, however, that in this extreme cold the charcoal can be reluctant to stay alight and we need to coddle the burners, keeping them warm until the heat is strong enough for the burn to continue.

POLLYANNA SKETCHES IN TEN-MINUTE BURSTS.

In the absence of wildlife, the huskies make delightful models. The dogs are not tame in the way our domestic pets would be considered tame - and most are very wary of us. One or two of the younger dogs approach us and sniff at our hands and allow us to stroke their heads and ears. Pollyanna is fascinated by their dense fur and mismatched eyes and has soon covered several pages with quick sketches, capturing their different characters in a few swift strokes.

The Inuit do not usually give names to the working dogs in the teams. With just one day of travelling behind us, we have named the lot - from here on in they will be known as 'Tangle', 'Fluff', 'Wolfie', etc. A pretty young female is christened 'Ginger', and the team leader 'Scarface'. The interaction of the teams is fascinating to watch - although 'interaction' is actually a polite term for fighting, the activity which occupies most of the dogs' time.

Whenever we stop for a break, the dogs firstly roll in the snow to cool down and then, tired out from the work of pulling the sledge,

'Interaction' between two Huskies.

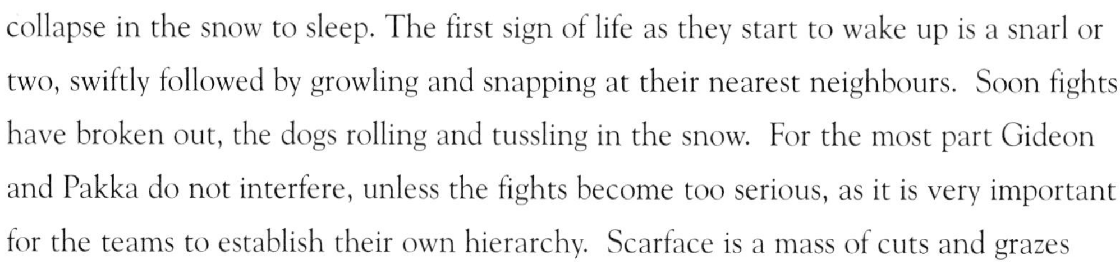

collapse in the snow to sleep. The first sign of life as they start to wake up is a snarl or two, swiftly followed by growling and snapping at their nearest neighbours. Soon fights have broken out, the dogs rolling and tussling in the snow. For the most part Gideon and Pakka do not interfere, unless the fights become too serious, as it is very important for the teams to establish their own hierarchy. Scarface is a mass of cuts and grazes from defending his position as the leader of the pack. Huge and very strong, he is almost all white, with a large brown patch on his back and brown ears, much bitten and chewed. Pakka tells us that the Inuit still leave the Husky bitches out when they are in season to be mated by the wild Arctic wolves, in order to keep the strain strong and tough. I have heard of this before, but had always assumed it was a myth told to gullible Southerners who ventured into these remote regions, for the future amusement of the native people. However, Pakka appears serious, and looking at Scarface, I could easily believe that he has a good proportion of wolf in his genes.

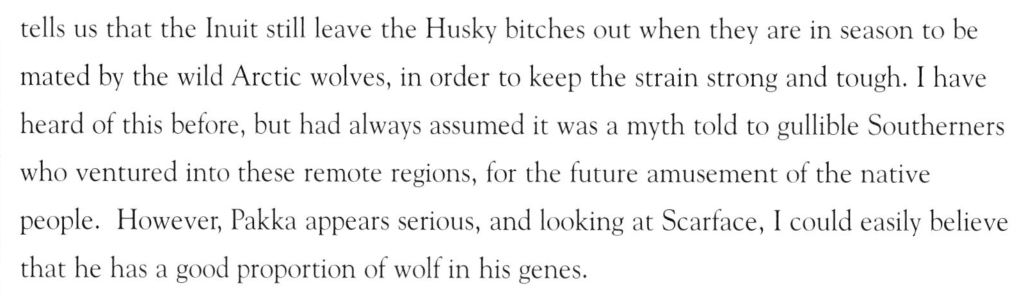

Scarface.

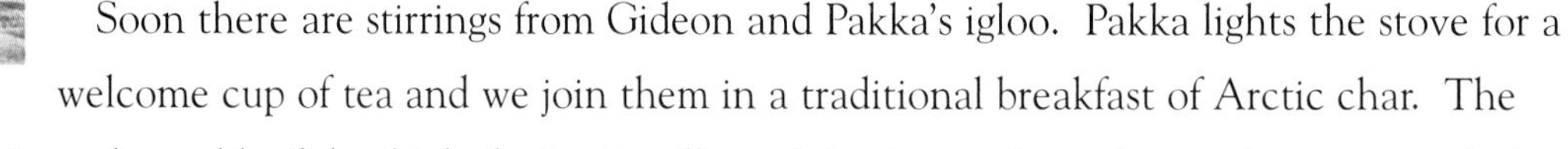

Soon there are stirrings from Gideon and Pakka's igloo. Pakka lights the stove for a welcome cup of tea and we join them in a traditional breakfast of Arctic char. The char is a salmon-like fish which the Inuit still catch in the traditional way - by cutting a hole in the ice and dropping a fishing line through into the Arctic Ocean below. The char is then prepared following an age-old Inuit recipe - it is served raw and frozen!

Breakfast quickly completed, we begin the preparations for leaving our campsite. We are finding any physical work extremely difficult in this climate. We can only move awkwardly due to our layers of clothing; but in these cruel temperatures mobility has to be sacrificed to body heat - our clumsiness and discomfort is the price of survival. We find that even the smallest tasks leave us tired and breathless, a sensation not dissimilar to the feeling of walking at high altitudes where the oxygen is thin - but we are literally at sea level. We can only assume it is caused by the unaccustomed

Study of Huskies.

The sledges are turned upside down . . .

coldness of the air that we are breathing. Although Gideon and Pakka are completely acclimatised to their home environment (and are wearing correspondingly fewer layers of clothing) they still move relatively slowly when carrying out their tasks. Pakka explains that they try to avoid any extreme physical exertion that could cause them to sweat, as the perspiration could then freeze on their skin. So we pack up slowly and deliberately. The sledges are turned upside down and snow and ice hacked off the runners where it has built up over the previous day's journey. The sledges will then travel more smoothly over the snow, making lighter work for the dogs and enabling us to cover more ground more quickly.

. . . and snow and ice hacked off the runners

With the sleds repacked, the Inuit turn their attentions to harnessing the dog teams. I attempt to help. The huskies attempt to hinder. Each dog pulls the sledge by means of a stout nylon rope attached to a harness. A 'draught strap' looped across the front of the sled holds the trace lines. The ropes are attached to the dogs' harnesses with a toggle fastening, that can be unhooked if necessary. In this region the dogs pull the sleds in a fan formation, so the ropes vary in length, with the team leader having the longest leash at fifteen metres, and the rest of the team progressively shorter ropes according to age and strength. As Gideon and

Team Spirit
Private collection (Hong Kong)

ᐊᐳᑦ

With the sleds repacked, the Inuit turn their attentions to harnessing the dog teams. I attempt to help.

Pakka struggle to attach the ropes the teams bark and snarl, fight and play, rolling around and weaving in and out, knitting the ropes into a complex macramé.

Eventually the sleds are loaded, the dogs untangled and we are ready to leave our first campsite behind. We have carefully gathered any litter, only our igloos remain. As the weeks pass and the days grow warmer, the sun will melt the blocks of snow, the frozen waters will thaw and the ocean waves will return once more - and there will be no trace at all of our brief presence in this imposing habitat.

Gideon tells us that we will continue to travel north, he hopes by the afternoon to have reached an area where we may find polar bears. We are travelling over the sea ice across Richards Bay into the Foxe Basin. The dogs move relatively slowly, pulling the weight of the sleds - around 8 kmph. The snow makes a soft cushion for the sled runners, but in places the wind has blasted the white covering away from the surface ice, which is exposed black and hard, causing the sleds to slither from side to side on the slick surface. On our first day we travelled for around five hours so we are already at least 40 km from Igloolik.

Untangling the leashes.

In the white infinity of this bleak wilderness it is impossible for me to grasp any sense of scale, or have any concept of north or south, up or down. Pollyanna tries to ask Gideon how he is navigating our journey. We have practically twenty-four hour daylight, so he certainly is not using the stars at any time. This close to the magnetic North Pole, compasses will not give a true reading. Travelling over the sea ice, under the immense curve of the Arctic sky the world is flat and white, entombed in permanent winter as far as the eye can see in every direction. Gideon shrugs. "We know the land", he tells me. He does not have the English to give more than this enigmatic reply, but he has lived in this area all of his life, as did his parents and grandparents, so he knows the way. The Inuit seem blessed with a sixth sense of direction, honed by constant practice. Hopefully this is true, if he is bluffing, and just guessing the route, I may never see a bathroom again.

A rare tender moment between two Huskies

It feels strange to have placed our trust so entirely in the hands of two people who are strangers to us, with whom we don't even have a language in common. If Gideon and Pakka were to abandon us on the ice we would have no idea of the direction in which to start walking to bring us back to Igloolik. In a jungle we could at least forage and

play Russian roulette with poisonous fruits and berries, but in this harsh environment we wouldn't know how to obtain food, or build a shelter. We would also be left entirely unprotected against a polar bear attack. Used to being independent and self-reliant this feeling of total dependency for even the basics of life is quite disturbing. Although our two guides have been unfailingly kind and polite towards us, we have both sensed a slight air of disapproval. We are travelling across the ice as men would, when on a hunting expedition. In a society where the women have as many as fourteen children, they are not expected to take on the roles of men. Not only are we therefore in the wrong place at the wrong time, but we are also of remarkably little practical help in this unfamiliar world. Like the construction workers back in Igloolik (an outpost of habitation which already feels more like a million miles away), our guides are probably expecting us to break down at any time and beg to be returned to the boarding house.

*Polar bears also 'know the land'. They are nomadic animals, following the patterns of the ice as it freezes, breaks up and thaws. Until recent years, biologists believed that polar bears travelled randomly all over the polar ice cap on top of the world, but it is now understood that they belong to approximately 6 distinct population centres and remain in roughly the same area year after year. The individual bears do, however, travel over an immense region and can range over frozen seascapes exceeding 32,000 km in area over the course of a year. Seals, the main prey of the bears, move from one area to another as ice and food conditions change; the bears also follow the changing ice. In order to hunt seals, they usually roam at the coastal edges, where sea meets land and the ice floes form. However, footprints of wandering bears, the true conquerors of this frozen world, have been seen within 2 degrees of the North Pole.*

A PECULIAR FALSE TWILIGHT HAS DESCENDED.

## DAY TWO (AFTERNOON): THE MAGIC KINGDOM

The blizzard which has been threatening finally arrives. Snow fills the ominous steel grey skies. Icy winds blast the flakes horizontally across the wilderness. The clouds are grey and forbidding and a peculiar false twilight has descended. We have no choice but to stop the sleds and batten down. Gideon and Pakka immediately start to construct igloos to shelter us, hampered by the appalling conditions. The huskies dig shallow hollows and, curling up, are soon almost covered by the blowing snow - little white bumps in a white landscape. The snow forms a blanket over their thick fur and helps keep them warm - a natural miniature igloo.

We have never felt so exposed to the mercy of the elements. Ordinarily we are protected from the harshest weather by buildings, vehicles, central heating, or air conditioning. Here there is no escape from the relentless buffeting of the gale and the coldness of the air. Back home snow falls in soft delicate flakes, drifting out of the sky, each one a unique combination of flat, transparent, hexagonal crystals of extraordinary beauty. This far north, these delicate crystals are whipped into round stinging pellets by the Arctic winds - hard enough to polish the surface of rocks into a smooth shine. The time has come to wear the fur parkas provided by Gideon. I sit on the sled, arms raised above my head and, for the first time since I left kindergarten, Pollyanna tries to help me dress, forcing the thick garment down over the layers of clothing, including the down-filled jacket. Pakka comes over to help, and eventually I am squeezed into layer No. 24. My arms are sticking out at right angles. I can barely move, which makes easing Pollyanna into her parka an even more difficult task. The effort proves worthwhile - the semi-cured skins provide an effective barrier against the wind-blown snow. My parka is made of caribou skin, the preferred choice for outerwear in the High Arctic. Caribou hair has a coarse outer layer covering a soft dense inner layer; the air trapped between them provides excellent insulation. Clothing is traditionally made from animals caught in late August and September, when the hair is the right thickness to provide the best insulation. When

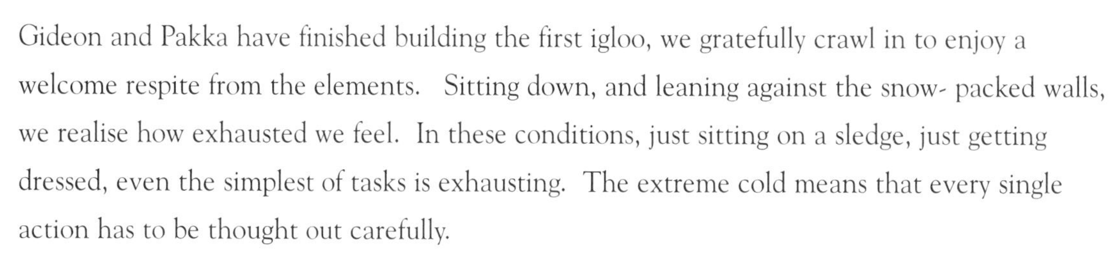

Gideon and Pakka have finished building the first igloo, we gratefully crawl in to enjoy a welcome respite from the elements. Sitting down, and leaning against the snow- packed walls, we realise how exhausted we feel. In these conditions, just sitting on a sledge, just getting dressed, even the simplest of tasks is exhausting. The extreme cold means that every single action has to be thought out carefully.

While we are curled up safe and sound in the igloo, Pollyanna continues to add to the sketches of the huskies that she began in the morning. Working from memory now, she adds more detail to the vague forms drawn on her paper. Even looking at these initial sketches I can tell that those who are lucky enough to see the finished paintings will be able to share in Pollyanna's Arctic journey, feel the sense of exciting discovery, experience another world through her work.

I sit and write my journal - like Pollyanna I have to work in pencil for the ink in my biro is frozen solid. I am seriously beginning to wonder why we ever thought it would be a good idea to venture into the Arctic. Despite travelling through some of the most strange and breathtaking scenery on the planet, it is so cold that my eyelashes froze together last night while I was sleeping. We have not seen even a hair of a polar bear, but instead have had to endure blizzards and snowstorms.

Eventually, Pakka reappears in the entrance to the igloo. He announces that the worst of the blizzard is over, the skies are clearing, and the snow has stopped at least for now. He is going to make some tea - would we prefer to stay in the igloo? We decide to step back outside to stretch our legs - and, on crawling out through the narrow entrance, find ourselves gazing round in wonderment. The sun has broken through the clouds and the air is full of tiny glittering needles of gold. We are in a dreamscape of minute, shifting, changing filaments of purest golden light. Within the hour, the Arctic has been transformed from a forbidding and desolate wilderness into a sparkling magical kingdom. I hold my hands out to try and catch the delicate shiny crystals, but they are too tiny and delicate to settle on the fabric of my gloves. Pakka is laughing at our delighted expressions, as we are transfixed by this beautiful natural phenomenon. He tells us that the Inuit call this effect 'diamond dust', a very appropriate name for the sparkling air. Apparently, the diamond dust only occurs in conditions of very extreme

cold, when the tiny moisture content of the Arctic atmosphere freezes in the air. For the first time since leaving Igloolik, I have spent a short time unaware of the intensity of the cold, totally captivated by the beauty of this strange and breathtaking world.

*The polar bears survive all that the Arctic climate can throw at them thanks to their unique coat. Their fur appears to vary in colour from purest white to almost yellow, but the colour is really an illusion, caused by the reflection of light. Individual hairs are in fact completely clear and hollow. Recent research has shown that the hairs trap ultraviolet radiation and conduct it - in the same way that an optical fibre conducts light – down to the skin. Scientists working at the University of Boston found that polar bear fur has an incredible 95 per cent efficiency when it comes to converting the ultraviolet rays from the sun into heat. The hairs trap light from every direction and then the energy flows in one direction only, towards the skin. This enables the bear to maintain its body heat. This phenomenon was first discovered when a group of Canadian biologists was trying to assess the extent of polar bear populations using aerial photography. Traditional photography was useless because the white bears blended so well into their snowy habitat. The scientists then tried infra-red photography, which detects the heat given off by warm-blooded animals - but this failed because the fur was such an effective form of insulation no outside heat could be detected. Only ultraviolet photography worked, because whilst the snow reflected back 90 per cent of the ultraviolet rays, the bear's fur absorbed them and provided a contrast on the film. The skin beneath the bear's fur is black, like its nose and lips. Beneath the skin lies a 8 centimetre layer of blubber, further insulation against the cold.*

ᐊᐳᑦ

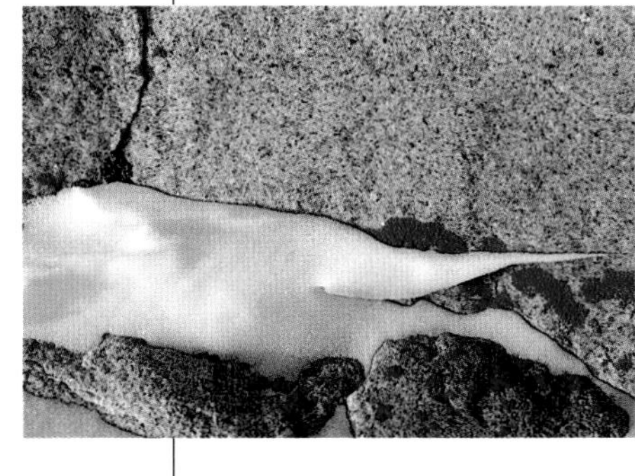

## Day Three: Beside the Seaside

Crawling out of the igloo in the morning we are cheered to find that the skies are still clear and the winds much subsided. The Arctic landscape is a sparking white tableau, the freshly fallen snows of yesterday's blizzards pristine and unmarked in every direction beyond our camp. When we are ready to move on it feels as though we are venturing afresh into the unknown, easy to imagine that we are the first travellers ever to set foot on unexplored lands.

As has been the pattern, Gideon leads with his eleven-strong dog team, Pollyanna on the back of the sled, Pakka and I follow on behind. The Arctic is eerily silent; the only sound the creaking of the sledge runners on the snow and the quick short panting of the dog team as they pull their heavy loads.

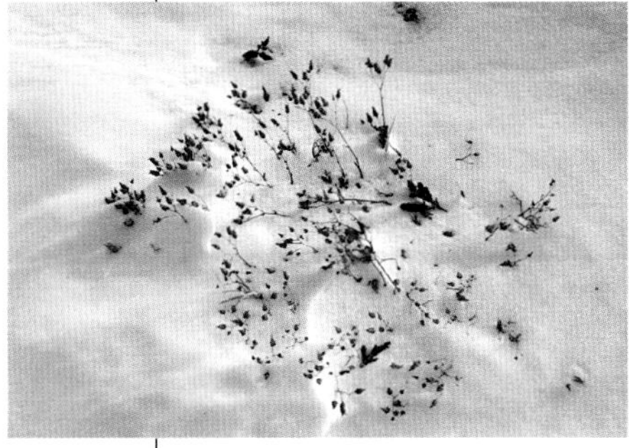

We make good time travelling over the sea ice and within an hour reach a different terrain - high cliffs of dark greenish-grey soapstone, as used by Inuit craftspeople for carving. Our route has brought us around to the edge of Ellesmere Island and for the next couple of days we will be travelling over land. In this strange environment, however, the difference between land and sea is not immediately apparent. Both are solid enough to travel over, and both are covered with a thick layer of white snow. Where the land meets the sea, however, there are wide swathes of 'barrier' ice, a chaos of pressure ridges, rough hummocks and jagged teeth of ice thrown up by the tremendous force of the tides, now casting long blue shadows in the Arctic sunlight. The frozen ocean appears to be one mass, but in fact it consists of countless thousands of individual ice floes, some hundreds of miles wide, some only a few feet across. These are constantly moved by the still-flowing backwaters of the ocean beneath and when these ice floes collide they are forced upward into steep ridges.

Several times the sledge has to be manhandled over the difficult terrain.

I had imagined that I would be relieved to reach solid ground once again - although the sea ice is around ten feet thick there is still something unnerving about imagining the black waters of the Arctic ocean still moving beneath the runners of the sledges. However, we soon discover that travelling on land brings its own particular problems. Large rocks protrude through the snow, making our progress jerky and halting. The sleds are not equipped with anything that could be described as suspension, so every bump and jolt is transmitted through

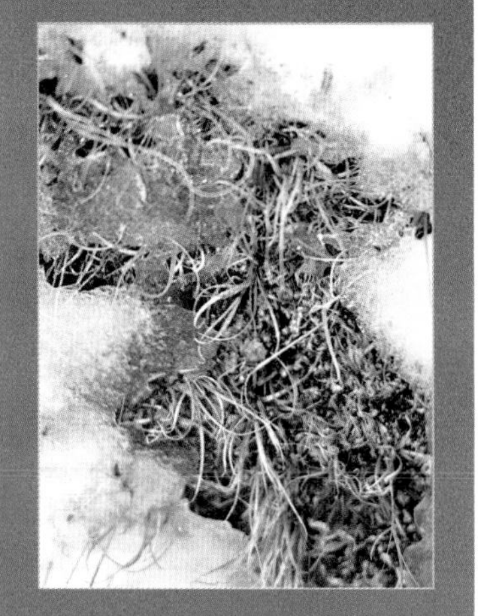

LICHEN SUSTAINS THE CARIBOU IN THE HARSH ARCTIC CONDITIONS.

the runners as we alternately bounce and slide along - even my incalculable layers of clothing cannot cushion the shocks. The dogs have to work harder to pull the weight over the uneven ground, so we cannot build up the same easy speed. Sometimes we encounter deep gullies and crevasses and *sastugi*. These are steep ridges of snow built by winds laden with ice particles. These wind sculptures have a beauty of their own, strange formations standing like the ruined remains of a wild architect's fantasy - but they do not make for an easy journey. Several times we have to climb down and help Gideon and Pakka manhandle the sledges over the difficult terrain when the dogs are unable to negotiate the route safely. We now understand why the land-fast ice floe is the preferred winter highway for skidoo and dog-team travellers. The ice covers the surface of all the coastal inlets and bays and grows as much as sixteen kilometres out into the open sea from the land's edge, creating a relatively smooth bridge between landmasses.

We have only been travelling overland for half an hour when we see that Gideon has stopped his sled a little way beyond. As we draw alongside, he points ahead. My heart leaps - have we found our polar bear? As I focus on the distant shapes before us on the ice, I realise that in fact Gideon has spotted a herd of caribou. Here in the frozen Arctic these animals eke out a meagre existence by pawing at the snow for the lichens, and grazing on the sparse Arctic grasses. As the herd approaches, I start fumbling for my camera. Photography in the Arctic is

THE HERD OF CARIBOU DISAPPEARS INTO THE DISTANCE.

not simple. My camera is buried underneath the top two layers of my clothing to prevent it from freezing. I have to remove my down-filled mittens and top layer of gloves in order to handle the delicate controls, all the while taking care not to touch the camera to my face so that the metal parts do not freeze to any exposed skin. Under these conditions changing a lens becomes a major ordeal, even simply changing film is an issue. The rolls of film freeze in the subzero temperatures, so I keep several rolls in my pockets close to my skin. If the film becomes frozen and brittle it can snap as I try to load it into the camera. When changing the films I also have to be careful not to exhale too closely to the camera or lenses. The moisture in my breath would immediately form into small ice crystals that could scratch the delicate surface of the film, or obscure the glass of the lens. The camera batteries are my kindred spirits - they do not take well to the cold either. Before leaving England we purchased special adapters allowing us to keep the batteries on leads, tucked inside our clothing, while the cameras are in use. Despite the additional warmth provided by nestling in my bra the batteries still only provide power for four or five films, and I am constantly replacing them.

The white-out glare of the unremittingly snow-covered landscape brings its own challenges. Left on automatic, my cameras assume the views are the usual mix of trees, buildings and grass - full of darker tones and shadows. The camera, therefore, under exposes the shots, producing films full of uniformly dark shots featuring grey snow and darkened skies. I find the quickest way to correct the exposure is to take a reading from a neutral grey card and adjust the settings according to this reading.

Unfortunately, I am overcome with excitement at seeing the caribou, our first live wildlife since leaving Igloolik, and grabbing my camera I shoot at random, trying to capture the large herd as they cross the frozen land. It is only as they are finally disappearing from view behind a rocky outcrop, that I lower the camera and realise my mistake. I quickly take fresh readings and adjust the cameras - but I am too late. The caribou have gone and I know all but my final shots, taken as the herd disappears into the distance, will be useless.

After a warming cup of tea we move on once again. Sensing I am a little disappointed, and still angry with myself after my failure with my camera equipment (what if Gideon had found a polar bear? Would I have no photographic record of it?), Pakka suddenly halts the dogs and

**CARIBOU**

**The caribou are remarkably well adapted to their Arctic environment. Their coat is so efficient at retaining heat that they are virtually impervious to even the worst of the Arctic weather. Caribou hairs are club shaped, thicker at the tip than the base, forming a densely packed outer layer, with tiny air spaces near the skin and within the fine curly wool underneath. The caribou maintains 2 internal temperatures. Its body temperature is stable at around 105°F, while that of its long legs is more than 50 degrees cooler. The veins and arteries in its legs are closely aligned, so that the out flowing blood transmits its warmth to the chilled blood that is returning to the heart. The blood vessels in the extremities constrict so that just enough blood flows through to prevent frost damage, but little of the precious body heat is lost to the surrounding air.**

**Each spring the female caribou undertake a remarkable trek back to the calving grounds, travelling up to 32 km a day, navigating across this vast and featureless land using memories retained from past migrations. Once they reach the calving ground, in mid-June, the females give birth to all the young within a 5-day period. Following this, the herds quickly re-group - for caribou there is safety in numbers.**

**THE ESKIMO HUSKY DOG**

**The Eskimo Husky dog is a breed quite distinct from the blue-eyed Siberian Husky, or the Alaskan Malamute. The dogs typically weigh 29 - 38 kg. The females stand around 50 cm high at the shoulder, larger males can reach a height of 70 cm. The dogs are built for strength and stamina rather than speed, with a thick neck and broad chest. Their dense fur helps to protect them from the cold, having a coarse outer coat over a shorter softer under fur. They have thick fur under their paws to protect their feet. Thick furry eyelashes help to keep the snow flakes out of their eyes.**

clambers down. He indicates that I should take his place at the front of the sled. Somewhat doubtfully I move forward. Has he decided that the time has come to release me back into the wild? To my relief he climbs up behind and starts to instruct me on the rudiments of sled driving. I am to shout "AYEEEEEE" if I want the dogs to move left, "HAAAH" if I want them to turn to the right, and "OY" to encourage them to move forward. I am handed the long leather whip. If I crack this at the side of the dogs they will move away from the noise and turn as required. While I am being given my first driving theory lesson the dogs have taken the opportunity to settle down in the snow and are dozing peacefully. We are ready to move. I clear my throat and shout "OY" just as Pakka does when he wants the dog to move on after a break. The dogs continue to snore. "OY!" I yell, masterfully. There is not so much as the flicker of an eyelid. **"OY!"** At the sound of Pakka's voice from behind me, the dogs leap up and start running as fast as their furry feet will carry them. Perhaps it is my accent.

We continue for another twenty minutes with me in the driving seat. I yell "AYEEEEEE" and "HAAAH" at intervals to attempt to stamp my authority on to the team and to steer us around any potentially dangerous rocks. The team does not show any discernible response to my commands, but continues blithely across the ice, navigating its own course around dangerous obstacles. Pakka should have provided 'L-plates' for the back of the sledge.

When we stop for our next tea break, Pakka gives me my second driving lesson, and attempts to teach me how to use the whip, a 3-metre-long leather strap, which he deftly whirls around his head cracking the end sharply as he brings it down to the ground with a forceful snap. My first attempts are sadly feeble, the whip swishing softly through the air and collapsing round my ankles, but after a little practice I am also able to produce a satisfying snapping sound.

I am allowed to practice my new found skill and drive the next stage of our journey. As usual Gideon and Pollyanna set out before us and ride ahead. Having the larger team of dogs they tend to travel more quickly, and often are completely out of sight, our dogs following the tracks of their runners. We only catch up with them when they stop, ready for a break or a welcome cup of tea. This time, however, we draw up to them very quickly. One of the runners on Pollyanna's sledge has slid into a narrow crevasse and is completely wedged. We join Gideon and Pollyanna hacking at the ice until we are ultimately able to free the stuck sled. When the runner is freed, Gideon urges the dogs to keep moving, so that they gain momentum and speed. This means that both driver and passenger have to run alongside and leap on while the sled is in motion. Gideon expertly springs on the front. Pollyanna misjudges her jump on to the back and keeps going, rolling right over the top and off the other side, much to her embarrassment and Gideon and Pakka's amusement.

DRIVING LESSONS!

I am starting to appreciate the fact that sled driving requires a great deal of skill and concentration, which goes some way to explaining the lack of conversation as we travel. Pakka needs to keep his full attention on the route ahead, to negotiate obstacles and potential hazards. Even the dogs' droppings are potentially treacherous; if the coat of ice which covers the sledge runners is affected, the sledge would become harder to pull, slowing our speed across the ice.

THE BEACH.

After another hour forging ahead we reach the area that Gideon has chosen as our camp for the night. On the beach. At the very edge of the ocean there is a semicircular inlet, surrounded by outcrops of rock. Climbing these cliffs which surround the bay we can see the shapes of the waves which appear to have frozen in motion as they rolled on to the land. As the entire vista is covered in a uniform layer of white snow it is very difficult to decide where the ground stops and the water begins.

Because the winds have subsided considerably since we started out, we are able to pitch our tents for the first time. Before we left home, we read many books about the Arctic region - largely about the wildlife and ecology of the area, but also accounts of the explorers and adventurers who had travelled through this desolate land. In many of the more recent books we had seen photographs of cheerfully grinning men, their beards encrusted with ice, standing proudly beside domed igloo-style double-skinned tents - impressive waterproof constructions in bright modern colours, with built-in ground sheets. Our contact at Canada North Outfitting had spoken to Luccassee before our arrival and had been assured that we would be able to borrow tents from the

OUR TENT.

Air-conditioning.

community and would not need to worry about providing our own. We had fondly imagined sitting snug and secure in these cleverly designed modern tents. We are, therefore, a little taken aback when Pakka and Gideon begin to unfurl sheets of discoloured canvas and lengths of wood. Our tents appear to have been abandoned in Igloolik circa 1920 by a passing scout team, and then seen a remarkable amount of use in the intervening years. The most modern feature they boast is the air-conditioning - provided by the tears in the canvas.

We attempt to help with the construction work. Erecting a canvas tent in the Arctic is not easy. Even the most prepared of Boy Scouts would struggle to pitch camp on an ice rink. Fortunately Gideon and Pakka are experienced Arctic campers. Instead of attempting to hammer tent pegs into the frozen unyielding earth, they turn the sleds upside down and tie the guy ropes around the exposed runners. Other fixed points are improvised. One of the frozen seals which is being carried for dog food is hammered nose down into the snow and used to anchor a shaky rope. Unnerved as I am by this macabre sight, I still cannot help but wonder what will happen towards the end of the journey when the dogs have eaten our tent pegs.

The tents are not in possession of ground sheets.

The tents are not in possession of ground sheets, so we are looking forward to a night spent sleeping on the ice. In the evening the temperature plummets and a deep cold pervades the air. I am glad that we brought bedrolls to lay under our sleeping bags. Furs are also provided to insulate our 'beds'. At these temperatures we need to be wrapped in at least twelve clos (cold weather units) of fabric to survive while we sleep. Thankfully we are also able to take the camping stoves into the tents with us - at least there is no danger of canvas melting overnight. Even with this heat source, the tents do not feel as warm as the igloos in which we spent the previous two nights. Although the stove heats the air, a thick layer of ice forms on the inside of the canvas as the condensation touches the thin barrier between our accommodation and the freezing Arctic air outside.

Our precious stove.

*Polar bears will occasionally construct temporary shelters in order to escape severe weather. Typically, however, it is only pregnant females that stay in dens for any sustained length of time. Usually these maternity dens are dug into snow banks, often on south-facing slopes near to the sea edge. The females use their claws to dig and smooth the interior, scraping snow away from the roof to allow a little light through. The dens consist of oval chambers, up to 1 m high, 2.4 m wide and 3 m long, with a smaller chamber down the slope that is vented to let the air circulate. Because of the insulating properties of snow, the heat given off by the bear may raise the inside temperature as high as 40°. On occasion a change in wind direction, or severe weather, may cause the roof of a den to become thin, or even to cave in making the den uninhabitable. In this event the female bear will leave and either dig a fresh den close by or take up residence in an unoccupied one. The females begin denning in mid-October or early November and remain there with their cubs until late March or April. Early naturalists' accounts of the great white bear were based on a mixture of fact and legend. In the 18th century the missionary Hans Egede wrote that the polar bears spent the winter months living luxuriously in huge snow caves "made with pillars, like stately buildings".*

A MACABRE TENT PEG.

## Day Four: Scarface in Love

I wake to be shown a new addition to Pollyanna's sketchpad. A cartoon of me, fast asleep in my sleeping bag. The fabric is gathered tight around my face, so not even a centimetre of flesh is showing, but as I breathe out, my breath freezes, sending out little puffs of fog into the cold.air.

This morning we discover another disadvantage to sleeping in tents rather than igloos. Temporary snow houses can just be left behind - they may be adapted as shelters by other travellers but ultimately, as the temperatures rise, the constructions will melt back into the ocean with the rest of the ice and snow leaving no trace of our passing. Tents, however, have to be dismantled, the frozen canvas folded and re-packed and loaded back on to the sledges. Thus, we make a considerably later start than we have on previous mornings. When we do set out the day is clear and bright, the snows glittering under the Arctic sun. Pollyanna comments that she feels that we have been here forever and I understand immediately - the 'civilisation' of towns and cities seems light years away. In this universe of silent ice I find it very difficult to conjure a convincing image of the streets of London or New York, filled with traffic, fumes and noise. Even the journey through Canada feels hazy, something experienced in a dream. In the frozen north day-to-day existence takes on a new intensity. The simplest tasks require careful consideration and planning. Keeping warm is a constant challenge. The continuing whiteness of this exquisite landscape is, at times, overwhelming, and time seems strangely distorted. It feels to us both as though weeks have passed since we set out from Igloolik.

As we travel onwards we still fail to find any traces of polar bears. When we first set out we were constantly watching for bears, but now it would be easy to forget the original purpose of the trip. The environment seems so harsh and barren that it is inconceivable that an animal the size of a polar bear could really exist here. Each time we stop, we still scan the land with our binoculars looking for bear tracks, but to no avail.

Now that we are travelling across land, however, we see the first signs of human existence since leaving Igloolik. We spot a cairn of stones sticking out of the snow, an *Innukshuk.* These large blocks of soapstone are arranged in a crude representation of a human figure - two

Innukshuks.

SNOWY OWLS

**These beautiful owls, their white feathers flecked with grey, are capable hunters, with a wing span of up to 1.2 metres. Even though they weigh only around 1.8 kg they are capable of catching a 5.4 kg Arctic hare. They also hunt ptarmigan and eiders, and have even been observed snatching char and trout from shallow rivers. Their staple diet, however, is the lemming and the population rises and falls in line with the fortunes of these small rodents. Females lay from 2 or 3 eggs to as many as 15 in a single clutch, incubating as soon as the first egg is laid. The young owlets hatch at intervals, the last often 2 weeks after the first to hatch.**

THE SNOW QUEEN
PRIVATE COLLECTION (UK)

upright blocks for the legs, a cross-piece representing the arms and a round boulder for the head. Pakka tells us that these *Innukshuks* are markers left by the Inuit to help travellers navigate the land.

We continue to follow the edge of the land, still apparently heading north, and through the course of the day come across several more *Innukshuk*. Pollyanna finds them beautiful in their simplicity, and is inspired to sit and make several sketches. Around the base of one of the constructions we find traces of a snowy owl - a feather, fresh looking pellets - but though we scan the area through binoculars, we cannot see any sign of the owl itself. It is impossible to imagine where they can hide in this open and exposed land, but even the sharp eyes of the Inuits, accustomed to searching the snow for wildlife, cannot pick out the shape of an owl.

We eat our lunch of frozen caribou sitting by an *Innukshuk*. The huskies roll in the snow and doze as is customary, but seem more restless than on previous days. When Pakka starts to gather their leashes in preparation for continuing the journey, the reason swiftly becomes clear. One of the young female huskies - which Pollyanna and I have christened 'Ginger' - is coming into season. Chaos ensues. Ginger is young and relatively unaccustomed to pulling the sled, so her leash is fairly short, positioning her at the back of the team while they are running. Unfortunately, the dogs who should be running in front of her are now more interested in running behind her. This results in much tangling of leads and a somewhat halting journey as the front-running dogs try to slow down and the sledge loses momentum over the ice. For the first time Pakka and I remain almost level with the lead sledge, occasionally pulling out in front. Gideon is becoming increasingly frustrated with his team especially as Scarface, his team leader, is as interested in Ginger as the other dogs, but is determined to keep his male rivals away from her. In the ensuing scuffle Scarface manages to chew clean through the tough nylon cord of Ginger's leash. Suddenly unencumbered by the weight of the sledge, and a little unnerved by the insistent attentions of her team mates, Ginger makes a break for freedom and races off across the ice at top speed. With a sudden jerk the sledge lurches forward. Determined to catch up with the newly irresistible Ginger, Scarface and the other dogs are pursuing her across the ice as fast as they possibly can. Pollyanna finds her sledge is travelling at far greater speeds than we have so far experienced.

Unfortunately, Ginger, rejoicing in her new found freedom, is not running over the ice in a nice straight line, but is zigzagging in haphazard bursts over the snow. Despite the shouts of protestation and sharp cracks of the whip from the Inuits, our sleds are following a similar course - with the two of us bouncing up and down on the back as we fly over the snow.

Eventually, a by now somewhat tetchy Gideon succeeds in stopping his sledge. The little brown shape of Ginger can be seen disappearing rapidly towards the horizon. Worried that we will never see her again, I ask Pakka if he thinks that they can catch her. He is quite surprised at the notion and he assures me that when we stop for the night Ginger will return to the team of her own accord. Dogs are, of course, pack animals by nature and after her brief taste of freedom she will be happy to return to the fold. The fold is already calling for her - lips pursed, heads thrown back, their frustrated howls and wails echo mournfully across the ice. Meanwhile, all four of us attempt to untangle the leashes knotted and twisted out of recognition after the afternoon's excitement.

When we pitch our tents that evening. Gideon tethers the dogs a little way from the camp as usual. Sure enough, within the hour, a little brown husky comes strolling out of the snow and rejoins her team, to the immediate noisy excitement of the males. Gideon tells us that he is quite happy for her to be mated, she is healthy and from a strong line - ideal stock to produce future sled dogs. We will be back in the village in just over a week and if she is pregnant she will not run with the sledges again until she has had her puppies.

*Female polar bears usually breed for the first time at 5 or 6 years of age. During the long breeding season, from late March until mid-July, an eager throng of fiercely competitive male suitors follow a female bear while she is in season – usually about 3 weeks. The sole parental responsibility of the male is to impregnate the female. After fertilisation there is a delayed implantation, meaning the embryo will not start to develop until September. Before entering the maternity dens the females eat heavily, seeking to double or even triple their weight. They most commonly give birth to twins, though can have between one and four cubs. At birth the babies are blind and helpless, not much larger than guinea pigs. After 2 months feeding on the fat-rich mother's milk, however, they will emerge from the den weighing up to 15 kg – around 25 times their birth weight. The cubs have a long childhood, continuing to nurse until they are 2 years old and denning with their mother for 1 or 2 more winters, occasionally staying with her for as long as 4 years. With a gap of 3 or 4 years between litters, some polar bears only produce young twice during their lifetime. Through DNA blood testing Canadian scientists recently discovered that some female polar bears will rear cubs which are not their own. It is unusual for wild carnivores to nurture and protect youngsters who do not share their genetic makeup. The scientists' conclusion was that the mothers were rearing the cubs out of mistaken identity - after meetings of family groups, the mothers simply did not recognise which cubs belonged to them!*

THE HOWLING
IN THE COLLECTION OF MISS K GADSBY (UK)

DAY FIVE: THE COMPANY OF WOLVES

For the first time Gideon and Pakka come to our tent before we are awake and call softly through the canvas for us to get up immediately. Blearily I crawl out of my sleeping bag, pulling on my down-filled jacket and reaching for my facemask, I try not to breathe the sharp, cold morning air too deeply. We have not slept well, having heard padding footsteps around the tents at night, which we assumed to be one of the restless huskies, loose from the pack.

As we fight our way out of the tent flaps, Pakka motions for us to be quiet. He points ahead to the rocky outcrops at the top of the cliffs. I see a dog-like shape. At first I think one of our huskies must have broken loose in the night. Gideon is hissing at me through clenched teeth and realisation slowly dawns - this is a wild Arctic wolf. I slip back into the tent to retrieve my camera – Pollyanna is already pulling sheets from her sketchpad to start work. The first shots I take are distant, as the wolf watches us warily from the shelter of the rocks. He is clearly aware of the human presence, but is not immediately running away from the perceived threat. The reason is obvious – the lure of Ginger is stronger than the fear of man. After pacing on the cliff for some time, the wolf eventually makes a run towards the tethered huskies only to lose his nerve as he nears the camp; he turns away sharply and flees rapidly over the snow, until we can no longer make out his pale form.

**THE ARCTIC WOLF**

**The white Arctic wolf travels far and wide in the barren lands of the Arctic, searching for prey. Travelling at speeds of around 8 kmph, the wolf can cover over 48 km a day. Although wolves usually travel in packs during the winter months, in spring and summer lone wolves will stray from the group and prowl the ice alone, allowing the pack to cover a much larger area in search of food. To contact other members of the pack the wolf will throw back his head and howl, the sound travelling for miles across the empty land. Arctic wolf pups are born in late May or June, usually in litters of six.**

THE ARCTIC WOLF FLEES THE CAMP.

A FEW USEFUL INUIT WORDS AND PHRASES

NANUQ
Polar Bear

AIVIQ
Walrus

ARARUQ
Wolf

QIMMIQ
Husky

ITJIQARVIK
Arctic

ARSANIQ
Northern Lights

PAPA
Food

IGALAK
Fresh Water Ice

IKKII?
Are You Cold?

NAMIIPPUNGA?
Where Am I?

UNA SUNA?
What is it?

IKAJUNGA
Help

We are thrilled. Over a cup of tea, I pour over the sheet of sketches Pollyanna was able to complete - the outline of the wolf captured in pencil on her watercolour paper. The Arctic wolf is a specialised sub-species of the North American grey wolf, distinguished primarily by their white coat and slightly smaller noses and ears. When we return to Igloolik, Pollyanna will add washes of colour from memory, bringing these simple pencil lines to life. Gideon and Pakka are amused by our excitement. I suspect that they are really thinking that it is such a waste for a new pair of wolf skin boots to have escaped over the ice, but they are under strict instructions from Luccassee not to hunt any of the wildlife while we are with them and only to use their rifles in self-defence should it become absolutely necessary.

When we first met Gideon and Pakka they seemed very unsure about taking us out on a sledge trip. I suspect that they were also a little worried at the responsibility of having to return these two helpless looking blondes back to the community alive and in good condition. There is no shortage of ways to destroy yourself in the Arctic and our inexperience in this climate must have been painfully obvious. Though both have been unfailingly polite, neither could be described as being particularly friendly so far. This morning, however, the barriers seem to go down a little - perhaps because we seem to be willing to help where we can, or because we seem to be genuinely interested in our surroundings.

Conversation remains somewhat stilted, however, as we do not have a full language in common. We have learnt pitifully few words in Gideon and Pakka's native language, Inuktitut that is spoken across the North West Territories. "Yes" (Ii), "No" (Aakka), "Thank you" (Qujannanniik), "I am cold" (Quuliqtunga) and bizarrely "Butterfly", which I can remember because it is such a delightful word – "Takilikkitaks". We have been told that Inuktitut is a very difficult language for outsiders to master. Apparently, the grammar and construction are very unfamiliar and many words sound and look similar, but can have very different meanings. Although both our guides speak reasonably good English, they are not fluent enough to allow lengthy conversation. So far our exchanges have been of a largely practical nature "Are you hungry?" "Are you tired?" "Would you like another slice of caribou?".

Travelling across the snow on the first day Pakka turned to me and enquired if I was warm enough. Despite the vicious Arctic wind I felt well insulated in my twenty-three layers of clothing and replied that I was fine, thank you. Pakka pondered this for a moment, then turned back to me and confided, "I'm frozen". I took that to be a bad sign. I had assumed that acclimatised as they were to this way of life in the snow and ice, the Inuit would not feel the cold. This exchange, though revealing, did give me cause for thought. If even Pakka was finding the temperatures uncomfortable, what chance did I have of surviving the trip?

This morning, however, the weather is better. Not only do we have some sun, we have seen a wolf and spirits are high. Gideon walks a few metres away from the camp and starts to dig in an unmarked area of snow. Some moments later he returns triumphantly with a frozen fish - a whole Arctic char. I am somewhat surprised - I had imagined that the Inuit obtained their seafood by fishing, not digging. Gideon tells us that he caught the fish on a previous hunting trip in this area and decided to bury it in case he came out this way again and needed more food. When I mentioned that I couldn't see a marker to indicate the location, Gideon shrugged and explained that there was little point in making a mark as in the intervening weeks between journeys snow would blow over and cover small stones, etc. It is obviously not worth constructing a more permanent *Innukshuk* to locate one small fish. When I enquire how, in that case, could he possibly remember where the fish had been left, I receive another simple but enigmatic reply, "I know". Our lack of common language does not permit further explanation.

A lone Arctic wolf peers at us from the saety of a rocky outcrop.

An Arctic char is pulled from the freezer!

Our party sets out that morning in buoyant mood, skimming across the ice, optimistically scanning the horizon for polar bears. Ginger is now running separately from the rest of her team, tethered loosely behind the sled so that she can run along behind us, out of reach of the male huskies, thus giving us a far less erratic journey than on the previous day.

Now that one Arctic predator had revealed itself to us, we were feeling sure that a polar bear could not be far behind. But by lunch break our confidence had dimmed a little, and by the time we pitch camp for the night, more or less vanished. We have spent another long day watching snow and ice and although Pollyanna's sketchbook is rapidly filling with huskies and wolves and even outlines of our tents and igloos there are still many blank white sheets waiting to be filled with images of bears.

Ginger

*Journals from early expeditions into the Arctic record polar bears as dangerous and ferocious beasts responsible for damaging equipment and killing explorers. Although polar bears do occasionally kill humans, generally speaking they only attack when provoked or extremely hungry. In the 1970s the Canadian Wildlife Service promoted safety for Arctic travellers with the slogan, 'A safe polar bear is a distant polar bear', advice which still holds good 20 years on. Polar bears have excellent eyesight and hearing at least equal to ours. Their sense of smell is so incredibly sensitive that they can detect a seal on the ice more that 32 km away. They can also sniff-out seal dens covered by 1 m of snow and ice. These extremely intelligent animals will employ basic 'tools' and have been observed using frozen blocks of ice to break into seal dens and even to kill their prey. One Manitoba-based researcher, Dr Charles Jonkel, once saw a polar bear push a large rock 30 metres across the ground onto the trigger of a live trap set for the bear. With the trap safely sprung the bear took the bait and ate at his leisure.*

Gideon and Pakka like to look at Pollyanna's sketches each evening once we have pitched camp. There is a great tradition of art in the Arctic, not in painting, but in sculpture. When we passed through Iqualuit, we saw many beautiful soapstone carvings, representing all the birds and animals found in the Arctic – from polar bears, seals and narwhals to tiny lemmings and snow buntings. It is believed that many of the older animal carvings, especially those of bears, represented the spirit helpers of the shaman - spiritual leaders and medicine men in the Arctic communities. The carvings would have formed part of the magical equipment needed to transport the shaman on spiritual flights to visit deities and implore their help.

Tonight, once the tents are erected, Gideon and Pakka take the precaution of running a tripwire round the perimeter of the camp for the first time. Apparently, we are now very much in polar bear country. The thin rope surrounds the camp around one metre from the ground, secured with small stakes and attached to the runners of the inverted sledges. I find it very hard to believe that this would provide any form of deterrent to a determined polar bear tempted by the smell of our caribou meat. In fact, the trip wire, if touched, would detonate a small 'thunder flash' thus scaring the bear and alerting our two guides to the danger. Pakka reassures me that the best protection we have is our husky team. If a polar bear were to approach the camp the dogs would act as an early warning system, barking and howling the minute a bear came within sniffing distance. This would give Gideon and Pakka time to arm themselves. If a bear did attack the camp they would initially fire warning shots into the air and there is every likelihood that the noise would scare away any bear instantly. They promise us that they would only shoot directly at the bear if absolutely essential, that is to save a life. For the first time it occurred to me that I wasn't so sure if I wanted to see a polar bear after all.

DAY SIX: WHITEOUT

Ice Ice Snow White Snow Snow Snow Ice Ice Iceberg Wilderness Whiteout Snow Snow Snow Ice Ice Snowdrift Ice Ice Sea Ice Snow Ice Ice Cold Ice Ice Ice Colder Ice Ice Snow Snow Snow Freeze Snow Ice Ice White Snowfall Snowflake Snow Snow Snow Ice Ice Icy Icebound Ice Ice Snow Icecap Glacier Ice Ice Snow Icedrift Snowdrift Freezing Wind Icefall Ice Ice Icefield Snow Whiteness Snow White Snowblind White White Whiteout Ice Ice Ice Floe Ice Icy Icier Iciest Ice Ice White Cold Chill Snowbound Ice Ice Ice Snow Chilled Ice Ice Snow Snow Ice Ice Cold Snow Coldest Snow Ice Ice Snow Snow Ice Ice Ice Ice Frozen Caribou Meat Ice Ice Another Slice? Ice Hot Hot Welcome Tea Ice Ice Icicle Glittering Sparking Glistening Glinting Snow White Snow Bright Snow Snow Snowfall Snow Snow Snowy White Ice Ice Frozen Snow Snow Snow Snowiness Ice Ice Iciness Ice Ice Snow Snowball Snowfall Ice Ice Ice Snowblind Ice Ice Snowbound Ice Ice Snow Wind Ice Snowfield Snowflake Snowfall Snow Snowline Ice Ice Snow Snowstorm Snow Ice As White As Snow Snow Snow Snow Ice Ice Icicle Cold Chill Shivering Ice Ice Numb Ice Ice Snow Chilling Cold Cold Ice Cold Ice Ice Ice Snow Snow Ice A Shape On The Horizon Snow Snow White White Whiteout White Bear? Snow Ice Ice Snow Snow Ice Cold Disappointment Ice Blind Blinding Snow Blindness White White Dazzling White Ice Ice Snow Cold Shivering Shivery Cold Cold Ice Ice Snow North Wind Blowing White Ice Snowing Ice Ice Snow White Light White Snow Unblemished White Snow Snow White Whiter Whitest Ice Ice Ice Driven Snow Ice Ice Snowflake Glacial Ice Ice Tent On The Ice Smooth As Ice Ice Rink Ice Ice Snow Snow White Snowdrift Ice Ice Snow Ice Ice Snow White Snow Ice Ice Frost Ice Frost Bound Frostbitten Ice Ice Snow Cold Colder Coldest.

The crystal Arctic landscape.

## Day Seven: Fear and Loathing in the High Arctic

When researching this journey, I read the following description of the Arctic, "the whole of the country has so hard and severe a winter that there exists for eight months an altogether insupportable cold" - only to find that these words were written by the Greek Historian Herodotus in 480 BC. Throughout our written history those of us who live in warmer southern climes have been equally fascinated by and afraid of the frozen north.

The weather has taken a downturn again today. Still not as cold as the day we first set out, but very overcast and grey, with strong winds whipping over the fallen snow. Again we travel all day through the monochrome landscape without a glimpse of a bird or animal.

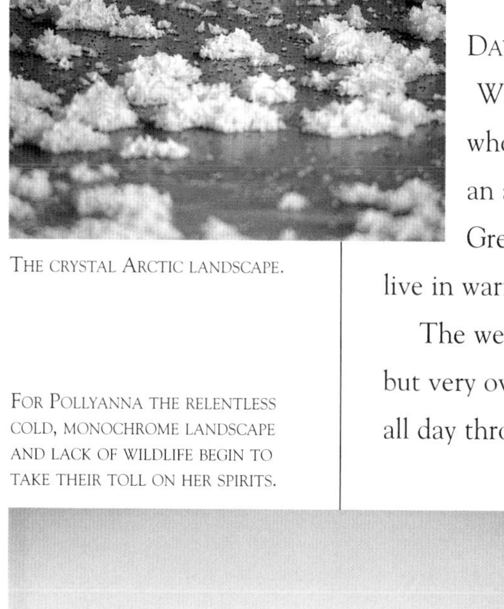

For Pollyanna the relentless cold, monochrome landscape and lack of wildlife begin to take their toll on her spirits.

My nose is now red and raw, the result of my inadequate mask. As we were travelling yesterday Pakka raised the whip and, bringing it snapping downwards, managed to clip the end of my already sore nose, the only exposed bit of flesh on my body. The pain was excruciating this morning and the skin is still very tender. I am developing a sore and itchy rash around my jaw line, caused by the constant rubbing of the coarse fleece lining the facemask. I try to soothe it with Vaseline and pad the inside of the mask with tissues to try and prevent the chafing, making me resemble Kermit the frog doing a bad impression of Marlon Brando as the Godfather.

After just one week we are becoming more blasé about the splendors of the crystal Arctic landscape. The vast expanses of drifting snow are no longer causing the gasps of awe they inspired a mere seven days ago. Under the grey skies the wilderness seems barren and depressing. We are frustrated by the lack of wildlife and very tired after a week of unaccustomed outdoor living in such extreme conditions. As Pollyanna has learnt over years of travelling the world to paint wildlife, the more 'natural' the habitat is for the animals, the tougher the conditions will be for her.

During the afternoon, I fall asleep on the dog sled while Pakka is

ᐊᐳᑦ

driving. This is in itself a fairly remarkable achievement. The sledges do not run smoothly over the ice and, despite the padding of the animal skins, the hard and lumpy packages strapped to the frame do not provide the most comfortable resting place. Despite this I find my eyelids growing heavy and with my legs still dangling over the side, I lean on the packing crate and doze for half an hour, the snow thrown up by the running dogs whipping past my face on the Arctic winds. I should, however, consider myself fortunate that I am not suffering from anything more serious than tiredness and a nasty little rash, because when we break for lunch (I'll take the caribou, thank you) Pakka describes some traditional Inuit cures for common ailments.

We had been concerned that the extreme change of diet would upset our digestive systems, but in fact we are both surviving our new raw meat diet very well. The fact that we have stopped thawing our food before we eat it, and changed from a ninety-five per cent vegetable diet (with an occasional piece of fish) to a ninety-five per cent meat diet (with an occasional piece of frozen fish) should have been enough to send our unwary stomachs into spasm. In our favour, the Arctic is at least a very sterile environment, the sheer cold killing off many of the germs and bacteria that attack hungry travellers in other countries. It is a blessing that our stomachs are coping so well, as the traditional cure for diarrhoea is to swallow pre-chewed caribou fat. The thick fat is chewed in order to start the breakdown and digestion of the yellowy substance, which is then poured into small bags (usually made from the whole foot of ducks or loons), to be kept handy in the Inuit First Aid Kit. This cure sounds worse than the disease.

When we pitch camp that evening I notice that Pollyanna is very quiet. As soon as the tents are secured in place, she wanders off and sits alone on a rock some distance away. I walk over to ask if she is feeling OK. No. She is not. She is not physically sick, but feels that she experiencing something akin to a panic attack. It is so big, so cold, so white out on the ice that she doesn't feel she can cope any longer. There is too much space, too much silence in this desolate sterile landscape trapped in an eternal winter.

I am very worried. This is very out of character. Normally Pollyanna is the one who is rushing ahead, full of enthusiasm, wanting to see everything, experience everything, constantly

## Arctic Cookery

### WALRUS CACHED IN GRAVEL

Take a chunk of walrus meat during the summer months. Cover with a generous layer of blubber. Place stones and gravel over top until entirely covered. Allow to ferment for several weeks. The blubber will saturate the meat giving a 'sharp' flavour.

*Note: if walrus meat is unavailable, fish can also be prepared using this method. The fish can be left to ferment for up to two summers, after which time it will attain the consistency of liquid cheese.*

### CARIBOU HEAD SOUP

Slice an oil drum in half to create a kettle. Fill with fresh water. Place caribou heads in vertically, turning occasionally.
Cook over medium fire for 2 hours, or more if required.

### SIDE DISH

Mix frozen ptarmigan excrement with seal oil. Serve immediately.

SAVOURY DIP (*AALU*)

Dice lean seal or caribou meat. Add drops of melted fat, and a few drops of blood. Add ptarmigan intestine (*uruniq*) to taste. Stir briskly with the fingers until the mixture has doubled in volume and is fluffy in texture. Can be used as a dip.

VEGETABLE SIDE DISH (*NIUKKAQ*)

Remove the stomach contents from a caribou. Freeze in a container until ready for use. Thaw, then gently knead the contents, carefully removing undesirable pieces of grass, lichen or leaves. (This process is called *siingijaijuq*.) Serve when the consistency is smooth.

*Note: These "recipes" are all devised from genuine common methods of food preparation in the High Arctic. However, I would not recommend testing them in other conditions. Should you decide to try your hand at Arctic cookery, please remember NOT to use the liver of a polar bear - it contains very high levels of vitamin A, and is toxic to humans.*

THE KITCHEN.

finding fresh inspiration for her work, often in the smallest detail unnoticed by most people. To see her suddenly so quiet and subdued and afraid to continue is very disturbing.

Each evening, when the tents are securely in place, Pakka and Gideon have rigged up a primitive system of wires and boxes and radioed back to Igloolik to let Luccassee know that everything is OK. They call these transceivers *uvaq*, an Inuit corruption of the English word 'over' heard so often on the airwaves. Most Inuit now carry these transceivers on hunting trips - a welcome safety precaution in a way of life fraught with danger. Even after travelling for seven days we are not so far from the community that we could not be reached in around twenty-four hours by skidoo. We have not travelled absolutely due north, but followed a more curving route, as Gideon and Pakka try to lead us into the most likely areas to find polar bears. Skidoos can obviously cover much greater distances in a day than a dog sledge and when they were first introduced to the northern communities the locals immediately praised them as the best invention ever - a life-changing piece of equipment. Although the skidoo is still much in use around the community of Igloolik, for many the initial love affair with them was beginning to fade. Many people were returning to the more traditional form of transport - a dog team and a sled. The Inuit had realised that skidoos can break down leaving their passengers stranded many miles from home. With a team of dogs mechanical failure is not a problem. With nine or eleven dogs, if one (or more) were to be injured the remaining members could still provide the strength to bring the sled home. Snowmobiles, meanwhile, are unable to find their own way home in a storm. Also, (and this was really something we were trying not to think about too hard as the weather worsened) if the worst happens, and a traveller becomes stranded on the ice, in an emergency it is possible to survive by eating a dog - but you can't eat a skidoo!

In a sense, I felt it was this harsh reality of survival in the far north that was contributing greatly to Pollyanna's state of mind. We were both unused to facing meat in its raw state, even wrapped in shiny supermarket packaging. Hacking our dinner in frozen chunks from the torso of a still clearly recognisable caribou had proved something of a shock. At home we feed our dog on a joyfully unidentifiable mush of 'meaty' chunks in gravy from a sanitised tin can. Here the huskies crunch into frozen seal meat, snarling and fighting over every scrap. We have left our pre-packed and ready-washed supermarket diet far behind, and are faced with the grim reality of having to eat in order to live, without the luxury of turning away from meat out of preference or squeamishness. Here the deep freeze is all around us, but the nearest supermarket is many hundred miles away. In many ways we feel we have travelled through time, as well as round the world. We are wearing partially cured furs and animal skins stitched together with caribou sinew and we are living on raw meat, much as our distant ancestors must have done. Luckily as visitors to this world, we are spared from having to catch our own food and, of course, have the luxury of thermal underwear.

THE ARCTIC LARDER.

Pollyanna wanted to travel in the traditional way, by dog sled, not only in the hope of finding polar bears, but also fully to experience their habitat and environment in order to convey it in her paintings. We have indeed found ourselves in a new habitat and it is so completely outside our previous range of experience that it is almost overwhelming. One of the biggest changes is the absolute silence. We have come from a world of constant background noise - radios, telephones, traffic, conversation, bird song - into a place of complete, profound, quiet. All we hear at night in the Arctic is a husky's occasional mournful howl hanging in the keen night air.

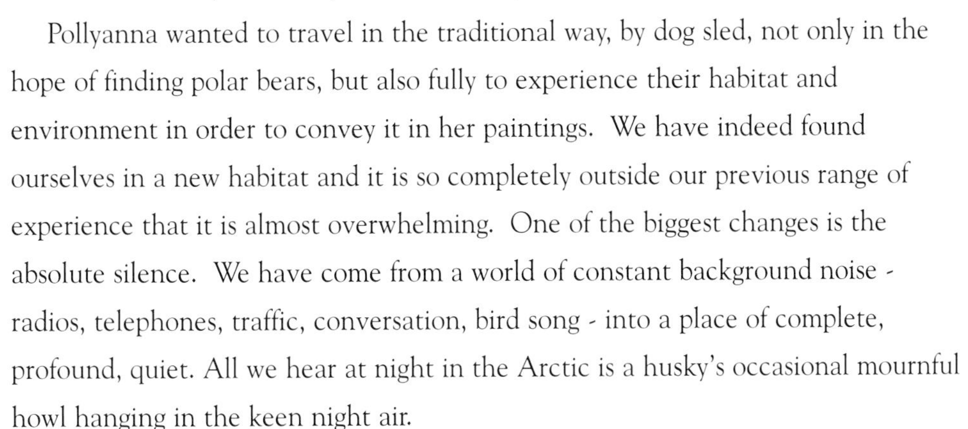

I know, however, that although Pollyanna is scared and depressed, exhausted by the travelling and disheartened by the lack of wildlife, that if we do give up and return to the community, in retrospect she would be hugely disappointed. I gently remind her how far we have travelled already, how much planning went into the journey. This situation of me giving a pep talk to Pollyanna on the verge of giving up takes us both by surprise. Before setting out we both assumed that I would be the one to give up - with my lack of camping experience, general dislike of 'roughing it' and extreme hatred of the cold. I thrive in hot countries (where Pollyanna has a tendency to wilt in the heat), but suffer in low temperatures. This unexpected role reversal goes some way to jolting Pollyanna out of her attack of fear. She agrees to press on for another twenty-four hours. If, by tomorrow

evening, she still feels that she cannot cope, we will ask Gideon and Pakka to radio the community and summon skidoos to pick us up, and whisk us back to civilisation.

In the event it is a very good thing that Pollyanna is prepared to keep trying for another day, because when we walk back to the campsite we discover that despite their best efforts Gideon and Pakka have, for the first time, been unable to make their radio system operate. They tell us that they will keep trying, but do not seem optimistic. The extreme cold is playing havoc with the batteries. I try to talk quietly with Pakka and explain that Pollyanna is feeling a bit depressed, and ask how long it would take if we were to use the dog sleds to return to Igloolik, using the most direct route available. He estimates four days. I decide not to share this information with Pollyanna at the moment. Pakka is sympathetic. Perceptively he asks, “Is it the food?”. I admit that it is not quite what we are accustomed to. Pakka’s face lights up. He signals that I should sit with Pollyanna on the edge of the sled. I do as instructed. Pakka rushes over to the cargo boxes and delves inside. I watch agog. Although we have not been specifically instructed not to touch the crates where all the food (with the exception of the frozen meat) is stored, Gideon and Pakka have made it quite clear that they do not really approve of us doing so. They are perhaps worried that, seized by hunger, we will eat all the trip’s rations in one desperate binge. We have, therefore, had to wait to be given welcome chunks of cheese (frozen solid as a brick) both sweet and savoury biscuits (frozen solid as a brick) and even squares of chocolate (you get the idea). I am so pleased to see the chocolate I nearly break a tooth. Realising that we are not as accustomed to frozen caribou as they are, they have on a couple of occasions boiled some chunks in a pan with water, making a stew which still tastes like a dish not so much past its sell by date as past its ‘feed to the cat’ date.

On this occasion Pakka emerges triumphantly with two cartons. With a flourish he removes the lid, pours hot water from the camping stove over the contents, stirs, peers in, stirs again. Beaming, he brings our evening meal over to us. It is a generic Canadian equivalent of pot noodle. I am speechless.

Caribou Stew.

The pot noodle is hot. It is not as chewy as frozen caribou. Therefore, it is unquestionably wonderful and spirits are suitably raised.

Halfway through my noodles, I am struck by how surreal our situation is. We are sitting on an upturned sled, on top of ten feet of pack ice surrounded by fields of snow. The only sounds are the baying of the huskies, tethered a little distance from us, and the occasional slurping of a wildlife artist and her daughter eating a pot noodle. I start to laugh, Pollyanna looks suspiciously at me out of the corner of her goggles. Clearly she is not the only one suffering from snow madness. Spluttering, I try to explain. Pollyanna joins in the laughter, probably more in amusement at my sudden attack of the giggles that anything else. Our laughter floats out over the frozen wasteland, the only sound of humanity for miles around.

*We may be finding it difficult to live in the harsh environment of the High Arctic, but the polar bear is a miracle of evolution, perfectly designed to survive the sub-zero temperatures. Zoologists estimate that polar bears evolved from their brown bear ancestors around 250,000 years ago, and have remained undisputed masters of this inhospitable kingdom ever since. It is estimated that there are currently between 7,000 and 20,000 polar bears roaming the Arctic - though some scientists believe that there may be as many as 40,000. The wide discrepancy of these figures demonstrates how difficult it is accurately to study these animals, which roam over such a vast uncharted and inhospitable landscape. After the war, pressures from hunting caused numbers to fall to an estimated low of 5,000. Polar bears now enjoy total protection in the Russian Arctic, and hunting is strictly controlled in the Canadian and Scandinavian regions, allowing the population to recover to current numbers. Today the biggest threat to the polar bears is caused by human greed. The Baffin Island region is rich in lead, zinc and gold, and possibly even diamonds - all waiting to be mined. Increased oil exploration in the Arctic Circle, and greater pollution from the highly populated regions to the south of their habitat, mean that the bears face the risk of slow poisoning, both directly from chemicals and by contamination of the seals which provide the major part of their diet. If increases in chemical contamination of the previously untouched ice fields continues at its current rate, polar bears will be officially classified as 'toxic' as early as the year 2005. Another major problem is the possibility of a massive oil spill in the region. Bears which came into direct contact with the spillage would almost certainly die as a result. The animals that survived would still be in danger from eating contaminated seals or birds. Left alone, polar bears will continue to roam their Arctic kingdom for another hundred thousand years, but we have to face the fact that a man-made disaster could wipe them out within a generation.*

The northernmost point of the expedition

I HAD FORGOTTEN HOW GOOD THEY TASTE!

## DAY EIGHT: FOR QUEEN AND COUNTRY

The changeable Arctic climate decides on dazzling white sunshine in piercingly blue skies. Everything is clearly defined in the crystalline air. Being English, we are naturally fascinated by all weathers, but we have never been in an environment where the conditions have had such a profound effect on mood - and potentially even survival. Pakka once again surprises us with a culinary treat. We are expecting to be faced with the familiar chunk of frozen fish for our breakfast, but from the deepest darkest recesses of the cargo box, Pakka triumphantly produces a packet of Kellogg's corn flakes. This is swiftly followed by a can of evaporated milk - he has thought of everything. The milk is frozen into a solid block inside the can, so we stand it on top of the stove until the liquid is thawed sufficiently to dribble out onto the bowl of corn flakes. I had forgotten how good they taste. We stand the can of milk back on top of the stove, and are enjoying our corn flakes so much we forget it is there until it erupts like Vesuvius.

As we drive the sleds onwards the Arctic once again appears magnificent and beautiful. The expanse of snow, blown into ridges and dunes resembles a desert of the purest, whitest sand.

That morning we are treated to a magical sight. A pure white Gyr falcon, the most beautiful of the Arctic birds, flies down from the clear blue skies onto a soapstone rock, only yards from us. He stops, swivelling his head, scanning the snow with piercing yellow eyes, before taking off once again, flying swiftly away and vanishing out of the range of our binoculars. I fire off half a reel of film - and Pollyanna swiftly captures the lines of the bird in flight on her sketch pad. She is fascinated by the idea of painting white creatures in a white landscape. Although white is technically the absence of colour, as an artist she sees many 'shades' of white in the hollows and shadows, in the feathers of the bird and the sunshine on the snows. For Pollyanna this colour-free landscape of crystalline ice is a blank canvas absorbing and reflecting a myriad of subtle colours.

SNOW FALCON.

When we stop for lunch, Pakka announces that we have now reached the northernmost point of our journey. From here we will turn and make our way back towards Igloolik, following a different route, tracing a large arc. As I am unlikely ever to travel to a more northern point of the planet we inhabit. I delve into my luggage, and retrieve a somewhat crumpled Union Jack, kindly given to me by the Canadian shopkeeper who sold us our sorrel boots - he could not believe we hadn't packed our flag in case of just such an eventuality.

I proudly walk over to a clear unsullied area just beyond our sledges and, finding a mound of snow, triumphantly plant the flag in the top. Pollyanna grabs my camera and photographs the moment for posterity, much to the amusement of Gideon and Pakka. Realising that this represents a great moment for us, they produce the culinary *pièce de résistance* from the travelling larder. Two frozen packs of frankfurter sausages and a loaf of white bread. The frankfurters are boiled in melted snow in the kettle and the hot sausages then sandwiched between two slices of still frozen bread to make a hot dog. To top it all off (quite literally) they have even thought to pack a bottle of ketchup, frozen solid of course - but by holding the neck of the bottle over the stove we can coax red rivulets out onto the sandwiches.

After lunch we turn away from the edge of the land we have been following and once more head out across the frozen ocean. Back on the sea ice the dogs run more easily, forepaws outstretched, noses high in the air. We start to see dark holes in the pack ice, and Gideon explains that these are *aglu*, air holes made by seals.

A couple of times, to our great excitement, we see the grey heads of harp seals poking through the surface, only to vanish back into the safety of the ocean depths as they hear the sound of the sleds approaching. The seals are so wary we are not able to get close enough for me to take any good photographs, but using her binoculars, Pollyanna is able to make a few sketches of these endearing creatures with their huge liquid eyes before they disappear under the ice. Pollyanna also makes copious notes alongside her sketches - the words combined with her drawings will help remind her of the colours, textures and atmosphere of the Arctic. Gideon and Pakka are also quite excited to have found the seals. They are of course the main food of the polar bear and so the more seals we come across the more likely it is that we will finally see our bear.

When we stop at our campsite that evening (a delightful choice - freshly fallen snow as far as the eye can see, no amenities of any kind), I am quite looking forward to my meal, following the variety we have suddenly been treated to over the past couple of days, so when I see slices

An aglu.

**THE SPIRIT OF THE SEA**

**In traditional Inuit mythology, there are 3 powerful controlling spirits: the Sea Spirit; the Moon Spirit and the Spirit of the Weather. Of these 3, the Spirit of the Sea was the most powerful and feared.**

**In legend, Nuliayuk, a young orphan girl, was courted by a sea bird. In order to escape the bird's attentions, the girl had her brothers row her to an offshore island. A terrible storm came up, and in order to save the boat, the brothers threw her overboard, cutting off her fingers when she attempted to climb back into the boat. These fingers became the sea creatures who live with her and guard her at the bottom of the sea. From her watery home, she reigns over all animals. If the Inuit break any of the strict hunting taboos she will punish them by keeping away the game animals so the hunting trips are unsuccessful.**

being slivered off the now decreasing block of caribou, my heart sinks.

While we half-heartedly chew, Gideon regales us with one or two of the traditional Inuit myths about the creatures that inhabit this strange and barren land. The *kiliguak* was an Arctic mammoth that used to roam the land in ancient times. These creatures have long been extinct. Legend has it that the *kiliguak* used to travel under the ground, with just its tusks showing above the surface. Even today, every now and again a traveller will return home full of tales of the two huge tusks he saw gliding through the snow towards him...

Not content with frightening their many children with tales of fierce polar bears and extinct elephants, the Inuit have also devised a rich library of tales of giants who will capture and eat unwary travellers and strange magical dwarves who live out on the ice and can vanish at will leaving only footprints. So that night, when we settle down in our sleeping bags, I am not only huddling in my tent in fear of a polar bear attack, but I have a whole new repertoire of myths and monsters to keep me awake through the Arctic night.

THE GREAT WHITE HUNTER

*For thousands of years the polar bear has held an almost magical significance for the Inuit who share its Arctic home. Many believed that the polar bears hear and know every word spoken by man. One ancient myth tells that polar bears were once a race of humans who took on the powerful shape of the bear by dressing in skins. At night they would return to their igloos and become human again. One day a curious Eskimo woman discovered the tribe's secret. The bear-humans were so angry that they threatened to kill her - and every other Eskimo they could catch. As though the world's largest non-aquatic carnivores were not frightening enough as a neighbour, legends also grew of magical monster bears -* Kuqqugiaq *was a bear-beast with ten legs that preyed on humans for food. However, according to a legend from the Chukchi Inuit of Siberia, the polar bear could also be thanked for the return of spring. They believed that winter was a huge and dreadful frost giant, who descended from the north to sleep on the land. People and animals were forced to flee and hide from the cold. Only the polar bears were free to move about. When a mother bear gave birth to a particularly mischievous cub, the youngster would crawl into the frost giant's nose, making him sneeze. Now awake, the giant became homesick for his family and would return to the distant north, allowing summer to return.*

ᐊᐅᑦ

DAY NINE : OBSERVING THE TABOOS

Today it is Canadian Mother's Day. I noticed the date while we were driving through Canada before our flights and managed to buy a card secretly while we were in Ottawa. In the Arctic it is very easy to lose track of the days of the week (and even the time of day), but I am fairly confident that this is Sunday and present the card with a flourish. Pollyanna props the card up in the tent, in pride of place beside the stove. We have already celebrated Mother's Day in the United Kingdom back in March. If Pollyanna organises the working trips properly, she should be able to fly round the world claiming cards and presents all through the year.

MOTHER'S DAY

The weather is still bright and clear with the morning skies casting a deceptively warm glow, for the air is once again very cold. Icy winds sweep the frozen ground, piling up snow crystals into the huge white walls of new snowdrifts. Before we leave our campsite, Pollyanna takes a short walk round the area, fascinated by tiny formations of ice blown by the harsh winds into strange shapes, natural sculptures in miniature. It is a privilege to travel through any new country with an artist: Pollyanna finds beauty in the smallest snow formations, seeing beautiful patterns in this white world which would pass unnoticed by the majority of people. She is constantly sensitive to colours, shadows and forms, viewing everything in terms of her art.

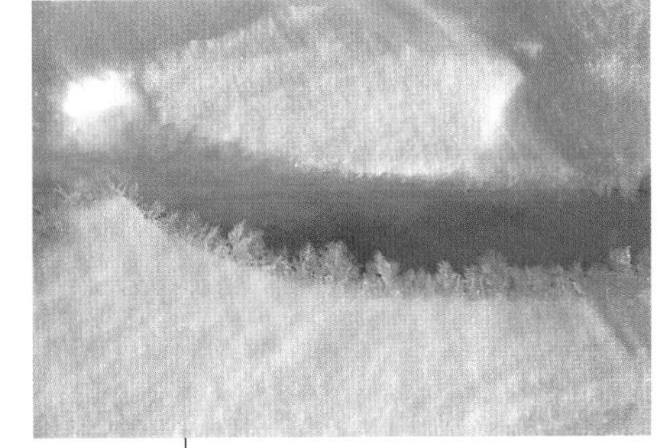

DEEP CRACKS IN THE THICK ICE LAYER.

In some places there are deep cracks in the thick ice layer. Some of these widen into crevasses and can be very treacherous. Ice crystals will form over the cracks and when the snow blows over the surface, they blend in perfectly with the rest of the ocean surface. A squeak from the ice field alerts us to the fact that Pollyanna has fallen into one of these crevasses. Fortunately, it is not one of the deeper ones, but she is wedged in quite firmly, almost to her armpits. It takes a good ten minutes for the combined efforts of Gideon, Pakka and myself to free her from this ice trap. Fortunately, she is not seriously hurt - her hip is bruised, and her shoulder is stiff (a frozen shoulder perhaps?), but she has not suffered any lasting damage. The incident is sobering, however, and we both resolve to be more careful while walking over the ice, testing the ground before we walk. Today we do not find any live wildlife. We do, however find the site of an unknown Inuit hunter's successful caribou hunt. All the meat has been taken, but some of the skin (which is not suitable for sewing into

CARIBOU ANTLERS ON A SNOW ALTAR.

clothing at this time of the year) is still lying on the ground, and the antlers have also been left, stuck into a block of snow. To me the scene looks almost like the aftermath of a ritual sacrifice, with the antlers a center-piece on a snow altar. Traditionally, Inuit hunters and trappers observed strict taboos and rituals out of respect for the creatures they hunted for food. They believed that all living creatures had a soul (distinct from a human soul, but a powerful life force none the less) and at death it would be reborn in another animal's body as long as it was treated with the utmost respect by the hunter at the time of death. Careful adherence to the multitude of rites and taboos which had to be observed would result in the soul of the animal conveying its good treatment at the hands of the hunter to other animals, who would then allow themselves to be killed.

In the earliest times it was believed that man could become an animal at will, and vice versa, with no difference between the two states. All spoke the same language. It is out of these beliefs that the hunting ethic grew and many hunters, even in modern times, will offer up profuse thanks to the soul of an animal for permitting itself to be killed and to provide food. In many Inuit tribes, when a hunter returned with a bear, complex ceremonies would be performed to appease the bear's soul, which hovered unseen around the community. The skull would be taken to the communal house and placed upon a raised bench, where gifts and offerings would be left. If a male bear had been killed the hunter would prepare dishes for the whole community for four days according to ancient tradition, such as *alluit* a mix of seal oil and berries and *tammogac* which consisted of reindeer tallow, dry fish, seal oil and water. If the hunted bear was female this part of the ceremony would last for five days. Then the community would perform the traditional intricate polar bear dance. Finally, the skull would be taken out onto the ice floes and placed on the shifting ice. When the moving ice made a noise, this was taken as the sign that the bear's spirit had departed.

It feels extremely cold by evening. Travelling at this time of year, we have practically twenty-four-hour daylight. We are a little too early for the true midnight sun - after its noon-time high the sun curves steadily downwards through the sky at a shallow angle and there is a darkening of the sky as it dips below the horizon for a mere twenty minutes or so. Although we never experience full darkness, there is a corresponding drop in temperature. For the first

### THE POWER OF THE NAME

The name was considered sacred in traditional Inuit society. At the time a child was born, a female elder attending the birth would utter a series of names of deceased relatives and the last name spoken at the time of the birth would be given to the child. If a boy received the name of his grandmother, his father would correspondingly address him as 'mother', his mother as 'mother-in-law', and his brothers and sisters would call him grandmother. He in turn, when he began to talk, would address them as 'my son', 'my daughter', etc. This confusing practice reflects the power of the name itself rather than a direct belief in reincarnation. If the infant should die before it is named, there is no mourning. A name can be changed several times throughout a lifetime, especially if it is believed that the person has become possessed by an evil spirit.

time, Pollyanna has lost the sensation in her toes, much to our concern. We set our tents up in record time and are quickly installed inside with mugs of cocoa, thawing out nicely. We were so cold when we arrived, however, that we forgot our precious cameras and left two of them lying unprotected out on the sled. They are both frozen solid, the lenses completely iced up. We cannot put them back inside our clothing in this condition - they could lower body temperature like a reverse hot water bottle. In desperation we hang the straps over the cross pole of the tent, suspending the camera bodies above the warmth from the stove. I suspect this is not recommended in the manual, but we cannot think of a better solution.

We are left with one working camera with which to record the spectacular sun glowing orange on the horizon at ten to midnight, washing the snow-blasted landscape with warm orange tones before vanishing briefly below the curve of the earth's rim.

THE SPECTACULAR SUN AT TEN TO MIDNIGHT.

*Polar bears are clever, patient and efficient hunters. They have been observed sitting motionless by a seal hole in the ice for up to 14 hours. When the seal surfaces for a breath of air, the waiting bear springs forward and grabs the animal's head in its jaws, killing it. The bear then uses its incredible strength to pull the seal, which can weigh up to 114 kg and have a diameter of 60 cm or more, through a hole just 25 cm wide, in order to feed on its prey. The bears will also stalk seals which are resting on the ice. When they are resting out of the water the seals always remain alert to danger, staying close to the water's edge and waking from a nap every 20 seconds or so to look around. Each time the seal drops its head and closes its eyes, the polar bear will inch slowly forward, 'freezing' again when the seal raises its head. Eventually, when it is close enough, the bear will charge forward at top speed in an attempt to grab the seal before it can slip into the water. The Inuit tell stories of polar bears covering their black noses with their paws, or even with snow, while creeping slowly towards seals, so that they will not be spotted. Sometimes the bears will approach from the water, swimming slowly towards the seal then submerging when they get close, rising from the water's edge to block the seal's escape route. Eye-witness accounts tell of the bears leaping 2 metres in the air from a swimming start to catch a seal on land. Any remains left behind by the bears are quickly scavenged by ravens, gulls or other bears. During the coldest months of winter the bears are often followed by a retinue of Arctic foxes, who rely completely on scavenging the leftovers for their survival.*

### Day Ten : In the Footsteps of the Great Bear

There is huge excitement when we emerge from our tent. Not more than five hundred metres away from our camp Pakka shows us a trail of huge prints. The flat oval imprints can only have been made by one animal - a polar bear. This is the closest we have come to the great ice bear since we set out. I immediately photograph the paw prints, and Pollyanna records them in her sketchbook, while Gideon and Pakka dismantle the tents with unusual speed. Fortunately, our cameras have survived their unorthodox treatment and are once again thawed out and working, so I am also able to take a couple of pictures. Gideon announces that we will follow the tracks as far as we can and, hopefully, find the polar bear - depending, of course, on the distance he has already covered since passing our camp on his nocturnal journey. A shiver runs down my spine to think that a wild polar bear has passed so close, apparently disinterested in our camp, his attention focused on his intended destination. I imagine him padding silently past us, paws crunching on the firm snow, his huge nose lifted to sniff the scents from our campsite. It is strange to think that we have been so close; the bear choosing to ignore the human interlopers in his vast domain, the humans sleeping and unaware of his huge presence.

I remark to Pakka that the huskies did not seem to make any more noise than usual during the night. He gives me a sidelong look which I interpret as 'Huskies! What can you do with

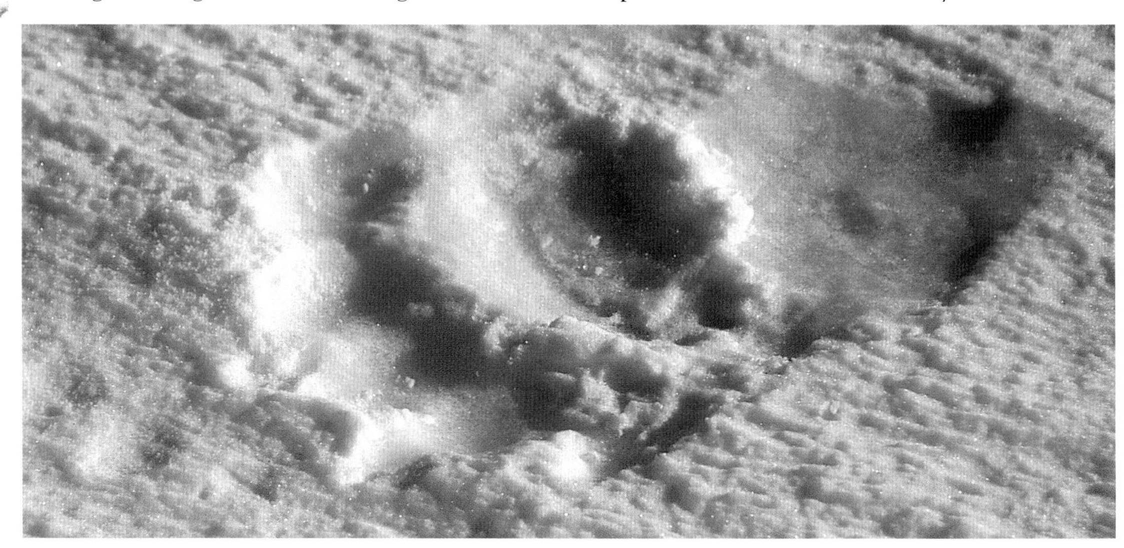

The footsteps of the great bear

THIS ICEBERG HAS A STRANGE TRANSLUCENT QUALITY, A COLD LUMINOSITY, ALMOST AS THOUGH A SAPPHIRE BLUE LIGHT IS GLOWING DEEP WITHIN.

them?'. The night always echoes to their intermittent howls and wails, the muffled sounds of fighting, eating and mating have become the backdrop to my dreams. If the dogs were more agitated than usual last night then Gideon and Pakka were no more aware of it than we were. So much for our early warning system.

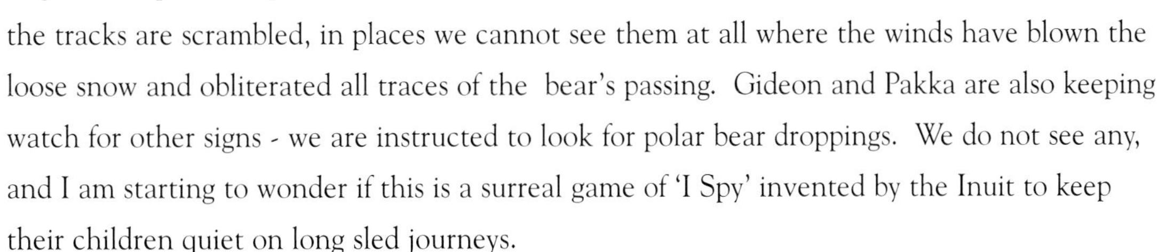

We help to finish the packing up as quickly as possible and start our journey, following in the huge footsteps of the polar bear. Here and there the tracks are scrambled, in places we cannot see them at all where the winds have blown the loose snow and obliterated all traces of the bear's passing. Gideon and Pakka are also keeping watch for other signs - we are instructed to look for polar bear droppings. We do not see any, and I am starting to wonder if this is a surreal game of 'I Spy' invented by the Inuit to keep their children quiet on long sled journeys.

Ahead, Pakka points to a massive block of ice rising out of the surface of the frozen ocean. This, he tells us, is an iceberg. When the ocean thaws out again in a few weeks time, the iceberg will once again float free. We can of course only see the tip, locked into the pack ice. The vast hulk of the iceberg extends into the still-flowing waters way below our feet. Icebergs are made of fresh water, land ice floating in the sea – huge slabs of frozen water broken free from glaciers. Pakka tells us that the older they are the more blue the ice appears. This iceberg has a strange translucent quality, a cold luminosity, almost as though a sapphire blue light is glowing deep within.

THE TIP OF THE ICEBERG IN THE KETTLE.

We stop the sledges close to this natural monolith for a warming drink. (On this occasion the tea is naturally made from the tip of the iceberg.) While I am drinking my hand slips and a drop of hot tea splashes out of my cup. By the time the liquid falls to my leg it has frozen in mid-air into a spike of ice.

Surprisingly, perhaps, the biggest challenge to Arctic survival is taking in enough liquid, so our tea breaks are frequent. The Arctic air is so cold it cannot hold moisture, so the human

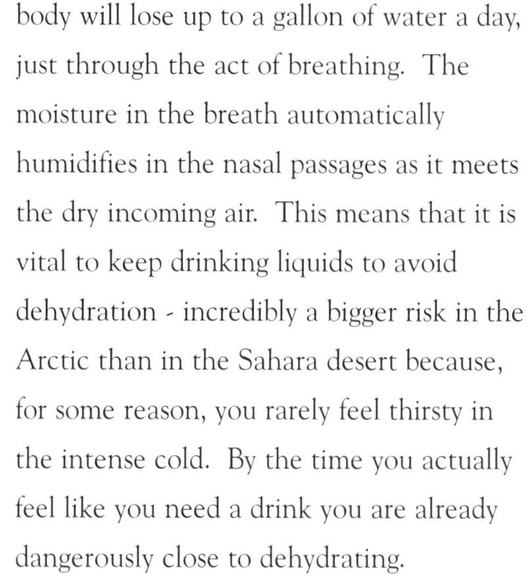

body will lose up to a gallon of water a day, just through the act of breathing. The moisture in the breath automatically humidifies in the nasal passages as it meets the dry incoming air. This means that it is vital to keep drinking liquids to avoid dehydration - incredibly a bigger risk in the Arctic than in the Sahara desert because, for some reason, you rarely feel thirsty in the intense cold. By the time you actually feel like you need a drink you are already dangerously close to dehydrating. Consequently, fainting and even heart attacks are common in the Arctic.

Pollyanna and Gideon finish their life-giving tea first and Gideon sets their sled in motion, heading out across the ice. Pakka is still clearing up the last of our tea things and making sure all the boxes and bundles are still lashed firmly to the sledge. I am leaning on the back, finishing the last drops of tea. Pakka hops on the front and starts to gather the whip. "Ready to go?" he asks. I take this as a general enquiry - have I finished my tea, am I ready to get myself sorted and leave and answer, "Yes I am." Pakka takes this "yes" as the cue to set out instantly. The dogs leap forward, at speed, and I am thrown from my precarious perch on the back of the sled.

I roll through the snow, fortunately well padded by my twenty-three layers of clothing, come to a breathless halt and pull myself upright only to be greeted by the sight of the back of the sledge still rushing ahead over the soft snow. Pakka's attention is obviously on the runner tracks ahead of him and steering his ever unruly team. He is completely unaware that he has lost his passenger. Further ahead I can see Gideon and Pollyanna's sled already lengthening the gap.

I am gripped by a moment of panic, even though common sense tells me that at some point Pakka will turn round to make some comment, or enquire after my well being, at which time he

is bound to notice the absence of a passenger. At the very worst, when the two sledges stop for their next tea break, someone, hopefully my mother will notice that I have dropped off. In the meantime though, I feel very small and vulnerable, standing alone in the shadow of the iceberg. Without human voices and the barking of the dogs, the Arctic is unnerving in its quiet stillness and I also find myself wondering about the polar bear whose tracks we have been following. Just how far away is the bear? I am alone, unarmed, and with no shelter. I am only too aware of my isolation, and of the frailty of human life in this vast unforgiving environment. In the silence nothing moves, apart from the occasional swirl of snow crystals lifted from the surface by invisible winds. I wave my arms helplessly at the diminishing shapes of the sledges. I am uncertain what to do for the best. Should I start to walk in the tracks of the runners in the direction the sledges are travelling? Or should I just stay by the iceberg, which is at least a clear landmark, and oddly comforting in its largeness. The idea of walking alone and exposed across the flat ocean is very unappealing.

Fortunately, I have no need to fear. The shapes of the sledges are getting larger. They have realised that I have gone AWOL already. It transpires that Pollyanna turned round for a last look at the iceberg through her binoculars and saw a little figure, waving. It took her a short while to attract Gideon's attention, as he was concentrating on the route ahead, and it is not easy to feel a tap in the shoulder though layers of fur, but she succeeded and pointed out the lone figure of her daughter.

This time when I clamber onto the back of the sled, Pakka waits until I am securely settled, and holding on firmly, before moving off.

*The polar bear whose footsteps we have been following will probably walk across 260,000 km sq of Arctic wilderness during his lifetime. In their poetry the Inuit call the bears* Pihoquhiak *- the ever-wandering one. The bears normally walk at a speed of around two and a half miles per hour, with a ponderous, rolling gait, only breaking into a run when absolutely necessary. They use a huge amount of energy in moving their massive bulk across the ice, and will frequently take the opportunity to lie down and rest. Their wide furred feet allow them to move through deep snow, but to save energy, they prefer to travel on solid ice or bare ground. When coming down steep hillsides, they have often been seen sliding down in the sitting position, using their extended forelegs as brakes. They have also been observed climbing steep ice cliffs and then 'sledding' back down on their stomachs, legs extended.*

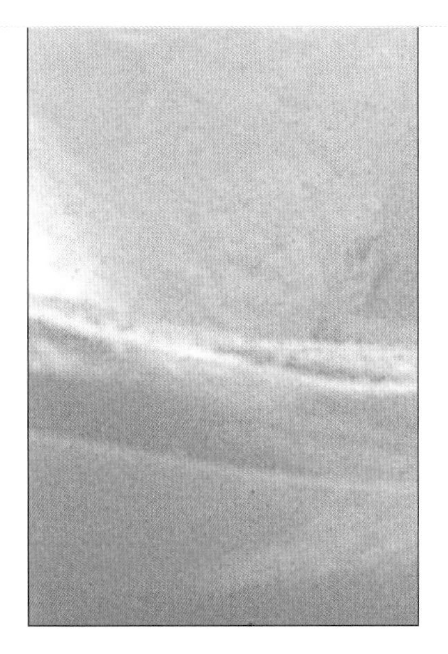

DAY ELEVEN: AT THE FLOE EDGE

Before we fixed camp the previous evening we had already lost track of the polar bear prints.

Gideon and Pakka were confident, however, that the bear was heading for the floe edge. Within two hours of travelling, on our tenth day out on the ice, we reach this same area. At the floe edge, the constantly shifting line where the frozen pack ice meets the Arctic Ocean, the seawater is a black, swollen mass, rolling, rising and threatening. Here the ice is thinner and it is possible to feel the movement of the tides below our feet. The ice is sighing and shifting as the deathly black waters roll underneath. Great sheets of ice are floating free out in the dark expanse of water that is only a few degrees above freezing. The ice all around us is creaking and groaning and I am concerned that at any moment I am going to find myself plunged into the ocean. Despite appearances this is not a beach on which the waves are gently lapping. Below us the freezing ocean is hundreds of feet deep; the natural environment of seals and polar bears which would be instantly deadly to us should we fall in. If the waters penetrated our clothing and reached our skin, hypothermia would set in almost immediately. Our flesh would freeze in four minutes, within seven we would be unconscious and death would follow in around fifteen minutes. Gideon and Pakka are no more protected against the ocean than we are, but seem very blasé as they walk close to the floe edge, peering into the cold, dark, deadly waters and watching for the movement of seals.

This area, where the ice meets the sea, is a favourite hunting ground of polar bears, because this is where the seals are at their most plentiful. I keep a respectful distance from the false shore, wary of the black icy unknown depths. Pollyanna and I sit on the sledges some twenty feet back from the edge.

While Pakka is preparing the stove for tea, Gideon suddenly halts and seizes his binoculars. In the far distance he has seen a movement. In this white landscape his sharp hunter's eyes have picked out a shape. He points. Pollyanna and I stare ahead. I can see... Nothing. After days seeing movement everywhere, spotting imaginary polar bears in every misshapen snowdrift, now that I am at last faced with the real thing, I cannot see it.

THE FLOE EDGE.

GIDEON'S SHARP EYES PICK OUT THE SHAPE OF A BEAR.

POLLYANNA HAS ALREADY REACHED FOR HER SKETCHPAD AND HER PENCIL IS FLYING ACROSS THE SHEETS AS SHE RECORDS THE MOMENT.

THE POLAR BEAR LAUNCHES HIMSELF FROM THE EDGE OF THE ICE.

Moments later I begin to make sense of the white forms ahead of us. There, alone, way in the distance, crossing the white wilderness is a large bear. This is the real thing. Not one of the lethargic, half alive creatures languishing behind the bars of a zoo, but a colossal wild Polar Bear, strong, lethal and unpredictable. He is walking steadily, purposefully towards the floe edge, his breath forming small clouds in the bitterly cold air. I am struck dumb by a sensation that balances on the thin line between wonder and fear. Pollyanna has already reached for her sketchpad and her pencil is flying across the sheets as she records the moment. Beside her earlier drawings of the footprints of this magnificent animal, she creates the unmistakable shape of the polar bear, so at home in his kingdom. In a few swift lines she captures the physical strength of the bear, his powerfully determined walk.

Gideon has reached for his rifle and is holding it loosely at his side, prepared in case the bear should unexpectedly change direction and attack our party. In reality, bears rarely attack humans, becoming fierce only when starving or provoked into violence. This polar bear seems to be intent on his course, and does not acknowledge our existence. As he reaches the water's edge he is only a few hundred metres away from us and I am able to shoot a few quick frames of film as he launches himself from the edge of the ice, diving into the dark waters, hitting the black surface almost side on. He dives down, leaving just one back foot breaking the surface of the water. Shortly afterwards his nose, and then his back, reappear some way further out. We watch in silence as he swims away, travelling due north, until we can no longer see the white form of his head in the dark waves.

The spell is broken, Pollyanna and I hug each other (as best we can given the clothing). The past few days have been challenging, at times frightening, and although neither of us had voiced the fear aloud, we were both convinced by this late stage that the we were not going to see the object of our quest, the magnificent polar bear.

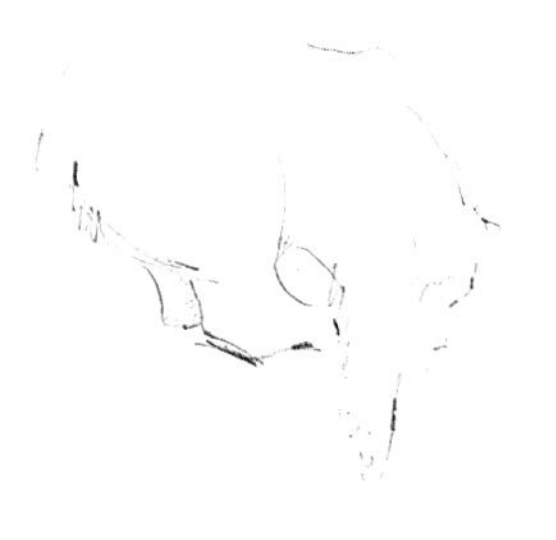

Ursus maritimus, *the sea bear, is an excellent swimmer and will dive into the sea to catch food or escape danger. Using their fore paws like flippers polar bears can swim for up to 95 km at speeds of nearly 9.6 km per hour, without resting. They have been spotted on ice floes 320 km away from the shore. The bears are able to see very well underwater and can remain submerged for up to 2 minutes with their ears flattened and nostrils closed, cruising though the water at a depth of 3 - 4.5 m. Some bears carefully slide into the water backwards, but others just leap head first from the edge of the ice. When they emerge they shake the water from their dense fur like a domestic dog.*

THE FLOE EDGE
IN THE PRIVATE COLLECTION OF MR AND MRS LAYTON (UK)

### Day Twelve: People, People Everywhere

From our camp, some 24 km south of the point where we had sighted the polar bear the previous morning, Gideon estimates that we are now less than a day's travelling from Igloolik. If we have a smooth journey, with no unforeseen problems, we should reach the community by early evening. Otherwise, we will have to spend just one more night on the ice.

Mid morning, Pakka slows our sledge. Up ahead, Pollyanna and Gideon have already stopped. We have company - the first human being we have seen since setting out twelve days ago. On a motorised skidoo, pulling a sled loaded with caribou, is a lone Inuit hunter. He has stopped to speak with Gideon and, as is traditional, share a slice of frozen meat. The hunter leans back on his sledge, which is heaped high with slabs of freshly deceased caribou, complete with antlers. Being English, Pollyanna decides to make polite conversation:

*Pollyanna:* "Good Morning"
*Inuit hunter:* "Good Morning"
*Pollyanna:* "Have you been out hunting?"
*Inuit hunter:* (Glancing at sledge piled high with caribou) "Yes"
*Pollyanna:* "What were you hunting? Was it caribou?"
*Inuit hunter:* (With another glance at sledge) "Yes"
*Pollyanna* "Did you catch any?"

At this point the hunter decides it is time to leave. We wave farewell as his skidoo speeds across the ice.

After two more hours of travelling, at the more sedate pace of husky power, we come to the Arctic equivalent of the M1. Close enough to Igloolik for people to travel out and back within a day, the ice is scored in a broad sweep with the runner marks of skidoos and sledges. Within minutes we meet more travellers, a whole family who are heading out on a day's ride - mother, father, and two children. Again we stop to share caribou, while the children, bundled up against the cold, play in the snow. This time Pollyanna sensibly restrains herself to smiles and nods. When the caribou slices have been duly finished both groups depart - our party

The Arctic M1

Inuit children.

Anna-Louise makes a friend.

A cameraman from the Inuit Broadcasting Corporation.

heading back to Igloolik, the family still making their way out towards the wilderness.

After the excitement of this unexpected human contact I settle down for the rest of the journey. My poor flayed nose is stinging with cold and I finally decide to give in to temptation and pull my facemask up to cover the raw exposed flesh. My goggles steam up immediately, as expected, and then freeze. I can now only see out of a very thin clear strip on the far right hand side of the mask. I don't care. My nose is warm. I have seen enough snow to last a lifetime. I am happy to spend the last few hours of travelling in a hazy fog.

I continue in happy oblivion for a couple of hours. After some time I vaguely detect the shape of a figure standing in the snow next to a skidoo. Pakka does not stop the sledge and I do not see him clearly. As soon as we have passed I heard the engine of his skidoo growl into life and he speeds past us towards Igloolik. Some time later I hazily see the same figure. Peering through my limited patch of clear Perspex it appears to me that he is holding a television camera. Pakka waves. I doubtfully wave as well. The skidoo sweeps past us once again. A short while later we pull alongside Pollyanna and Gideon's sled - they have been completely out of sight for some time. Pollyanna is standing beside the sledge. In front of her is the mysterious figure with the camera and she is speaking animatedly into the lens. As we swish to a halt the figure lowers the camera and extends a hand towards me. He introduces himself as a cameraman from the Inuit Broadcasting Corporation. Apparently since our arrival in Igloolik the community has shown great interest in Pollyanna's visit to paint the bears in their Arctic habitat and he has come out to record our homecoming. The Inuit hunter we met earlier had arrived back in Igloolik some hours ahead of us and informed the station of our imminent arrival.

Joy. I am about to make my debut on Arctic television. I am wearing twenty-three items of clothing. I am spherical. My nose is a scarlet triangle. I have not seen make up in days, let alone a hair drier. I put on a brave smile, and let Pollyanna do the talking. The cameraman films some of her sketches and takes a few shots of the huskies. Before returning to Igloolik ahead of us he asks if we would like to visit the IBC television studios the following day to watch his piece being edited for one of their general interest magazine programmes. We are delighted to accept. We are to discover that the studios consist of a medium-sized wooden

IGLOOLIK – A WELCOME SIGHT.

shed, boasting an array of ancient VCR equipment and a few monitors. The IBC network must cover one of the largest broadcasting areas in the world - but with one of the smallest viewing populations.

We now know that we will reach Igloolik within an hour and a half. Finally, knowing that we will not be in the tents that night, I allow myself to start anticipating warmth, a bed with sheets and, above all, a SHOWER. I happily sit back and fantasize about arriving at the boarding house, rushing straight into the bathroom and standing under the stream of warm water for an hour.

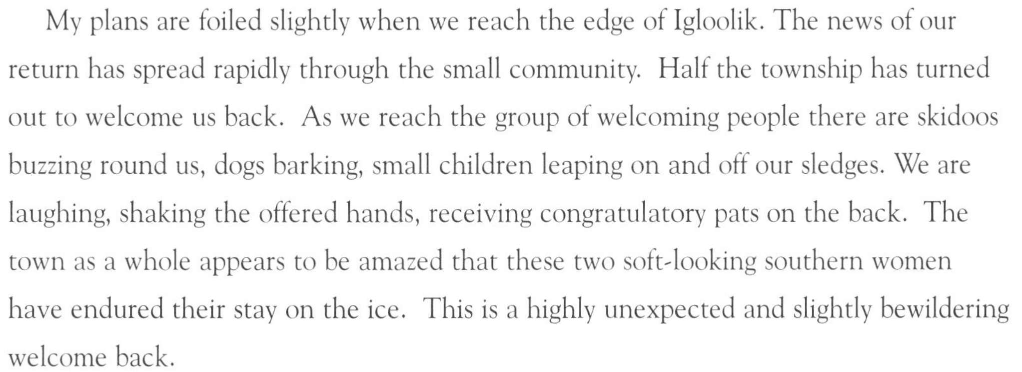

My plans are foiled slightly when we reach the edge of Igloolik. The news of our return has spread rapidly through the small community. Half the township has turned out to welcome us back. As we reach the group of welcoming people there are skidoos buzzing round us, dogs barking, small children leaping on and off our sledges. We are laughing, shaking the offered hands, receiving congratulatory pats on the back. The town as a whole appears to be amazed that these two soft-looking southern women have endured their stay on the ice. This is a highly unexpected and slightly bewildering welcome back.

THE IBC STUDIOS.

So, it is considerably later than planned that I finally reach the shower back in the boarding house. We have been out on the ice for just under two weeks, but it feels like a lifetime ago since we were preparing our equipment to leave.

Later, clean and dry, and feeling strangely light, moving without the encumbrance of twenty-three items of clothing, we sit at the kitchen table leafing through Pollyanna's sketch folder, as we sip glasses of orange juice.

Without ice.

ORANGE JUICE . . . WITHOUT ICE.

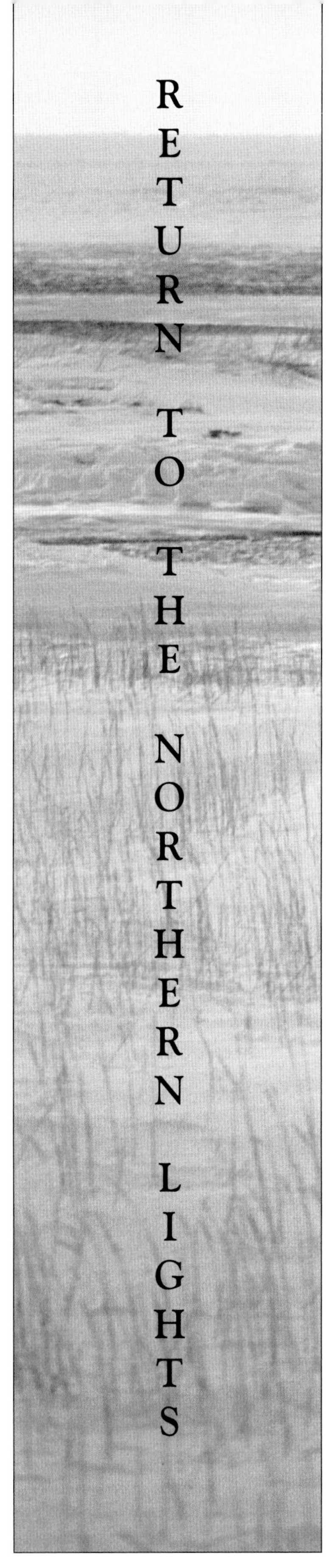


## *Chapter Four*

OUR first journey into the frozen north was magical and inspiring, but also harsh and physically draining. Pollyanna found enough inspiration in the unique beauty of the Arctic landscapes and wildlife to paint a highly acclaimed exhibition 'On Top of The World', staged in 1993. Our encounter with the huge male polar bear while travelling through his Arctic realm in the most traditional and natural of ways was an experience that will remain with us both for life. However, we were secretly disappointed not to have seen more wild polar bears.

In the spring of 1997 Pollyanna began to talk about the possibility of a return to the Arctic. The intervening five years had not completely obliterated memories of the biting cold, the sensation of the inside of the nose freezing with each intake of breath - but she was keen to try once again to sketch and paint the magnificent polar bears. We had reluctantly ruled out a visit to the famous polar bear town of Churchill when planning our first expedition, in order for Pollyanna to experience the wilderness of the world above the Arctic Circle. Now, however, the lure of a town which not only promised large numbers of visiting bears, but also hotels and boarding houses with beds and bathrooms was too great to resist.

After some initial research, I made contact with an American travel company, Natural Habitats, who have organised trips to Churchill for many years and have an extensive network of contacts in the area. They were happy to organise our flights and lodging - and also to make contact with the White Whale Lodge. Located some miles north of the town of Churchill, this is a research facility mainly used by naturalists, scientists and visiting students from the Saskatchewan University who are studying migrating mother bears with cubs.

So, in late October 1997, we find ourselves on board a small plane flying from Toronto to Winnipeg. My camera bag nestles comfortably next to Pollyanna's rucksack of sketching materials - between them they are taking up all the space in which we would normally sit - so we spend a cramped and uncomfortable two hours perched on top of our seats. During the flight, high above the clouds, glorious sunlight streams in through the plane windows. At Winnipeg airport the plane descends gently through the cloud cover - and lands in horizontal

THE FLIGHT TO CHURCHILL.

sleet. We check in at our hotel and, with the rest of the day to spare, decide to visit the Museum of Man and Nature. The museum boasts an impressive series of tableaux (according to which man primarily interacts with nature by killing it in various ways) and even a full-sized replica of the *Nonsuch*, the ketch which sailed into Hudson Bay in 1668, returning to England with a series of furs, ultimately resulting in the founding of the Hudson Bay Company. The museum is also superheated. We are dressed for a chilly autumn day in Canada. Pollyanna is on the verge of passing out, so we head for the entrance and step out into the cool air. Make that the freezing air. We step back into the sauna. And out into the freezer. And so we dance back and forth, back and forth, until our cab arrives to return us to our hotel.

The following morning, we fly up to Churchill - the small plane is not carrying any vegetarian food and the lunch-time snack is a sandwich which appears to contain at least six varieties of meat. I catch Pollyanna watching in amused disbelief as I delicately tweeze slices of beef, ham, turkey, roast ox, etc out of my roll, to be left with a limp lettuce leaf between two slices of bread. If my memory of Arctic cuisine is accurate, it will be the most edible food I see for some days.

POLAR BEAR ALERT.

Our landing in Churchill is slightly alarming - there is a thick fog and horizontally blowing snow, resulting in very low visibility and very high turbulence. The pilot comes onto the intercom to announce in a cheery voice that we should not panic if the first approach to the runway is 'misdirected' and he would then be forced to make a second pass at the airfield. Apparently, in this event, the plane is likely to 'shake violently' and make some 'strange noises'. I have never had a fear of flying, but it is not too late to start. We land safely, if a little bumpily, on the first attempt. When the plane doors open, a familiar shock of icy air rushes in.

In Churchill we meet up with Jason Bantle a zoology student at Saskatchewan University, who is paying his way through his master's degree by working part time for Natural Habitats. He is currently completing a thesis on Arctic foxes ("polar bears are bigger and sexier, but the foxes are just so damn cute") - and he will be flying up to the White Whale Lodge with us. We hop into his ancient rattling minibus and are delivered to our motel. The bus has no heating and whilst driving Jason is forced to thaw out the windscreen by holding the palm of his hand

CHURCHILL AIRPORT.

against the glass in order to melt the thick crust of ice which keeps forming on the outside, so that the wipers can clear a big enough space for him to see the road. We are staying at the delightfully aptly named Polar Inn - luxury! Our room has two double beds, a television, an *ensuite* bathroom, even a fridge, should we possess anything we wish to keep colder.

Originally, we had planned to travel straight up to the White Whale Lodge the next morning, but Jason tells us that there are around sixty male polar bears currently in the Churchill region. This is too good an opportunity for us to resist and Jason arranges for us to ride out in a tundra buggy the following morning.

The tundra buggies are very impressive. They were designed by a resident of Churchill, Len Smith, specifically for the purpose of safely viewing bears. Len built his first buggy in 1979 and he still operates Tundra Buggy Tours Ltd - the biggest tour operator in the town. Huge high wheels raise the square metal bodies of the vehicles safely above the reach of the polar bears. Sliding windows open to allow photography. The buggies are heated, and even equipped with basic rest rooms. There is a small outside 'deck', where we can brave the icy air for an unobstructed view of bears. We are introduced to Norm, who will be our driver for the day, and he handles the immense vehicle with apparent ease, as we leave the outskirts of the town, heading out across the flat snow-blasted tundra.

Churchill grew in an environment where three habitats meet - the ocean, the Arctic tundra and the northern tree line of the Canadian forests. It is believed that humans first settled in this area as long ago as 1700 BC - rings and other artefacts have been found by later settlers. The first Europeans arrived many centuries later, searching for a trade route to the spice rich Orient. In 1717 Captain James Knight established a trading port for the Hudson Bay Trading Company and the town of Churchill grew. Today it remains an important Canadian port. A railway into Churchill was completed in 1929 and the first ships loaded with grain left the port in 1931. The Inuit who hunted in this region in times past called it 'The Land of the Polar Bears'.

A TUNDRA BUGGY.

The distribution of both polar bears and seals in this area is influenced by the patterns of ice freezing and breaking up in the Arctic. The Hudson Bay is a huge pear-shaped body of water, around 1,290 km long and 1,600 km wide. During winter the bay freezes over

The last trees in Canada.

and the polar bears roam on the frozen surface, hunting for seals over one hundred miles out on the ice. In the milder temperatures of spring, the sea ice begins to thaw and break up. The bears find themselves riding huge chunks of ice, blown south until they reach the coast. During June and July the bears disperse inland and by the end of summer are beginning the long trek north around the bay, often some nine hundred miles, to wait for the ice to start forming on the north western coast once again. The big freeze starts during the cold days of autumn, when the air is still and the surface of the water chills below freezing point. First comes a slushy porridge of fine crystals, which gradually hardens to a fudge-like consistency. Within hours this hardens to become a brittle 'toffee'. Continued frosts cause further freezing and thickening - within a few weeks the ice can be forty centimetres thick and strong enough to take the weight of an adult male bear. By mid-October, up to one thousand bears can be found in the one hundred mile stretch of coast between the Nelson and Churchill rivers, the largest concentration of polar bears to be found anywhere in the world. As soon as the first hard freeze of winter occurs, the bears will begin to disperse out over the frozen bay in search of seals. Worryingly, here in Churchill, the bears may be feeling the first effects of global warming on the fragile Arctic ecosystem. The sea ice has been melting earlier each year, a trend which has only been broken once in the past fifteen years. This can deprive the bears of up to a fortnight's valuable hunting and feeding time each year, leaving them vulnerable to starvation. Less time to hunt on the sea ice means fewer reserves of fat to sustain them through the long and hungry months of summer. The area of the Arctic Ocean that is covered by sea ice dwindled by six per cent between 1978 and 1995. However, a study of sonar data

The view from the tundra buggy.

from naval submarines has shown that the ice cap may have shrunk by as much as forty percent in the last few decades. The sea ice is on average 1.8 m thick; thirty years ago it was 3m thick, a very significant reduction. If global warming continues at this rate, scientists predict that within fifty years the ice cap at the North Pole will actually melt each year - and by 2100 could have disappeared completely.

The landscape at the edge of the Hudson Bay is very different from the terrain we travelled across in the High Arctic. The snow blows across ice fields, but areas of stony ground are still visible in places and rivers run out towards the bay, still flowing through the frozen land. The bare branches of stunted willow trees stick though the snow, black against white, and at the edge of town the occasional spindly fir tree marks the edge of the tree line between the forests and tundra - a great contrast to the treeless barren lands we previously journeyed through.

We have only been travelling across the snow and ice for an hour or so when two young male polar bears stroll casually across the ice fields in front of our buggy. Although the pads of their huge furred feet are adapted for walking on snow, they are slipping and sliding on the smooth surface, seemingly oblivious to the giant vehicle ahead of them. This is the most wonderful opportunity for Pollyanna - in the warm interior of the vehicle she can use watercolours to add washes of colour to her sketches. She immediately begins work on one of the sheets of handmade watercolour paper she bought with this journey in mind. Pollyanna rarely works on pure white paper, but in the Arctic it provides the ideal background for studies of the wildlife. These sketches will form the basis for a second collection of work inspired by the Arctic. One glance at her working sketches will bring back strong memories of sights, smells and sounds experienced at the time of making the drawing. Few of her paintings are exact reproductions of a scene; they are a combination of sketches and experiences.

The only sound in the buggy is the clicking of my camera as we watch spellbound when the two bears rise up on to their hind legs and spar playfully with one another in the crisp Arctic light. Most of the bears in this region are male and the younger bears have been observed forming friendships which can last throughout the weeks until the bay freezes over. Associations can continue for years as they walk the ice, challenging our previous perceptions of them as solitary creatures roaming the tundra in isolation.

These two bears push each other with their huge paws, wrestling and embracing, all the time reining in their immense strength and power, so as not to inflict any actual harm. After a few minutes they drop to the floor, this entrancing spectacle of a mock fight, which brings to mind a waltz of sumo wrestlers, is finished. When it is clear that their demonstration of sparring is over, Norm suggests we move on. I cannot believe that he will drive away from two bears, but we follow his advice. He is familiar with the number of bears in this region and within a mere twenty minutes we see our third bear. A huge lone male is walking steadily across the ice, followed just a few minutes later by three younger males walking together. Norm stops the buggy to allow us to sketch and take photographs - still hardly believing that such an opportunity exists, to drive ignored amongst these magnificent animals in their homeland.

Next we find two young males, chewing desultorily on old dried out caribou bones. One of them heaves himself onto his huge feet and ambles over to the tundra buggy for a closer look. He sniffs the tyres, then rises onto his hind legs to sniff at the windows. I am only feet away from him and, despite the barrier of metal and glass, find that I am holding my breath. The bear realises that he cannot get inside for a closer look and drops back to all fours, swaying lazily back towards his companion, to chew on the caribou bone once again.

The light is beginning to fade, and Norm turns the buggy back to Churchill. In the evening glow we spot a beautiful Arctic fox, trotting delicately across the ice on dainty paws, round black eyes shining out of a snow-white winter coat. Beneath this luxurious fur is a surprisingly small animal, weighing a mere 4.5 kg. To round off an amazing day we even get a sighting of a male caribou almost silhouetted on an icy ridge, his antlers jagged black against the evening sky.

THESE TWO BEARS PUSH EACH OTHER WITH THEIR HUGE PAWS, WRESTLING AND EMBRACING, ALL THE TIME REINING IN THEIR IMMENSE STRENGTH AND POWER, SO AS NOT TO INFLICT ANY ACTUAL HARM.

Our room at the polar motel seems very inviting. Even today many of the residents of Churchill have never travelled more than fifty miles from home. Each year they play host to visitors from around the world - scientists and naturalists, artists and photographers, wildlife-loving tourists - all drawn by the remarkable opportunity to view polar bears on the edge of a town which grew up in the heart of the bears' traditional migration route. The bears that

Pollyanna will paint are following a route traced by generations of their ancestors for many thousands of years before the arrival of their human neighbours.

The inhabitants of modern-day Churchill go to extreme lengths to protect themselves from the bears who visit the community each year. Doors and windows are built strong enough to keep out a starving and determined bear. We see houses with welcome mats of nails - polar bears always test the ground before putting their full weight forward, so the sharp points will deter them, but not injure them. Nail-studded windows and doors appear to have been decorated by the itinerant designer of a medieval torture chamber and give a surreal appearance to the otherwise welcoming painted wooden buildings.

The following morning Norm collects us before sunrise and we climb up into the buggy to bump and lurch our way out over the ice. We spot our first bear of the day just as first light is appearing. He crosses silently in front of the vehicle - followed quickly by a second male, breath steaming in the dawn light. The Arctic light entrances Pollyanna. As an artist she is fascinated by the effect of the rays of the early morning sun highlighting the crisp white snow - she enjoys playing with light and shadow in her paintings and she often depicts her subjects back lit, or lit from unusual angles. The quality of the light in her painting is sometimes as important as the animal subject.

We sight a red fox, native of the forested areas, walking at the very northern edge of his range, hunting along a small line of stunted willow trees. Norm then drives us out to the very edge of the bay, where we spend the day in the company of four young bears. During the long wait for the ice to start forming the bears pass their time by sparring with each other (as beautifully demonstrated for us on our first day) - and by sleeping. We watch these young bears roll and stretch, curling up on the ice, biding their time and conserving their energy until they can once again hunt. They have scraped the surface snow away and are lying on the mosses, lichens and kelp, which compost slightly, giving off a meagre amount of heat. By this time of year, the bears have not eaten for several weeks, living off their immense fat resources. Seeing the bears resting languidly on the ice provides Pollyanna with

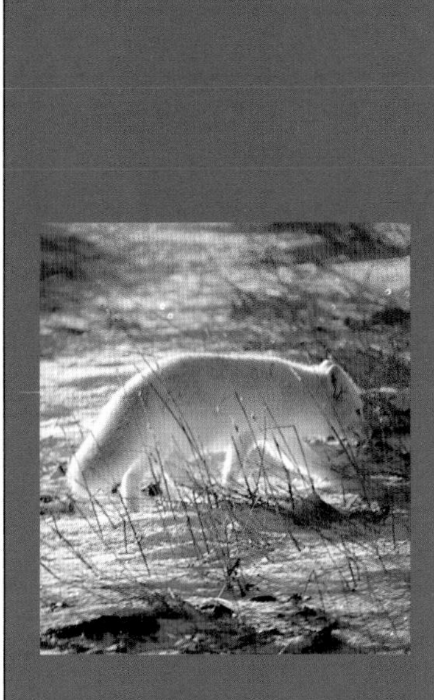

**THE ARCTIC FOX**

**Arctic foxes are smaller and silkier than the European red fox, with tiny rounded ears and a thick bushy tail. In summer their coat is grey brown, to blend with the tundra rocks and vegetation, in winter the coat becomes pure white to provide camouflage in the snow. They live by hunting for lemmings, smaller birds, hares and scavenging from the kills of polar bears and other Arctic predators. Opportunistic eaters, in leaner times their diet will even include seal droppings, beetles, worms and dead fish washed in by the tides. They breed in April, producing litters of 5 or 6 cubs. In a good season, when food is plentiful, they may rear the first litter and go on to raise a second before the end of summer.**

'Freshly canned people.'

a wonderful opportunity to sketch. Often when working with wildlife, she only has a split second to try and capture her subjects, but these bears are not going anywhere until the ice floes form - and she is able to complete detailed drawings. Each of her paintings is inspired by personal experience and contact with her subjects. In the months to come these polar bears will be brought to life again in her studio.

One of the bears is morosely chewing on a sprig of kelp; it is unlikely that he will obtain many nutrients from this small find - he is most likely chewing out of boredom. At this time of year the bears will scavenge whatever they can find to supplement their fat reserves - rodents, eggs, even berries. Since the arrival of man this summertime diet has been extended to include the occasional skidoo seat, tyres, or a carelessly discarded rubber boot. I am suddenly aware that to an acutely hungry bear the writing on our tundra buggy must read 'freshly canned people' - fortunately the bears know from experience that they cannot penetrate the huge vehicles and usually regard them with indifference.

Although we feel safe and protected within our near-armoured vehicle, we are about to be given a sharp reminder that despite the fact that the bears look like gentle giants while dozing on the ice, they are in fact the most powerful of Arctic predators. A fifth bear, which we had not previously noticed, is approaching from the north, walking purposefully towards the vehicle. He makes a careful inspection of the wheels, close enough for us to see his breath steaming in the freezing air. He sits down on the snow, directly below the back window of the buggy. Peering down at him, we can literally see the whites of his eyes. Without warning, he rears up to his full height and slams an enormous paw into the glass. We fall back instinctively away from the impact. Thankfully the window is made from toughened glass and doesn't shatter - but with one powerful blow the bear has reduced it to a spiders' web of cracks.

The window of our tundra buggy.

Making our way back to town we pass Churchill's notorious polar bear jail. This is a holding facility for bears that wander into the town and could pose a threat to the local population. Gigantic bear traps on the edge of town are used to humanely catch any bears drawn to this outpost of humanity. Stories abound in Churchill of polar bear attacks and the locals are more than delighted to regale visitors with hair-raising accounts of near misses - and the odd fatal attacks. Norm tells us of the most recent serious attack - a local man, a little the worse for wear, decided late one evening to deliver some raw meat across town to his sister. Unwisely, he slipped the parcel of wrapped meat inside his coat - thus effectively baiting himself and tragically attracting the attention of a roaming hungry bear.

Asleep on the kelp.

There are three residents currently languishing in the jail - we cannot see them, as there is a strict policy of not allowing human contact with these wild bears. They will shortly be tranquillized, scooped up in giant nets and flown out beneath helicopters to the barren ice fields far north of Churchill. All the bears are tagged before release, so any subsequent recapture can be logged and information gained about their migration habits.

Polar bear jail.

Nearing the edge of town, Norm stops the buggy near a team of huskies belonging to Brian Ladoon, who keeps his dogs tethered out on the ice a couple of miles from the town. We are able to pet and stroke them with ease - they are much more domesticated and friendly than the dog teams that drew our sledges on our earlier expedition. Apparently, bears will occasionally visit the team, but far from attacking these captive dogs, can be seen playing with them.

Returning from the buggy to the motel we pass by the harbour. The last ship of the season is being loaded with a shipment of Canadian grain bound for Ethiopia - the sea ice is already rapidly forming around the prow and this ship will soon be entirely icebound. We are told that smaller boats will try to clear a passage through to open water for the start of its long voyage.

Although it is tempting to remain in Churchill for longer - the guarantee of seeing polar bears so easily is a huge draw - we are determined to stay with our original plan and visit the White Whale Lodge. The following morning finds us joining Jason to load a minimum amount of equipment and clothing into the helicopter that will fly us across the broad Churchill River to the lodge. Once again I am wearing a ridiculous number of layers of clothing - but this time because it is the only way to transport my wardrobe, due to space and weight restrictions in the helicopter.

A female husky and her pup.

The flight is spectacular. The Arctic light is clear and the views of the tundra from above breathtaking. We are fortunate enough to spot a female bear leading two young cubs around a ridge of ice. The female bears usually follow a different migration route

Grain ship bound for Ethiopia.

from that of the males. Adult male bears will view cubs as potential competition and, during the lean summer months, even as food. While the males wait in the choice areas by the beach for the winter freeze, the females follow a longer but safer route inland.

The White Whale Lodge is located in the heart of the female bears migration route. As we arrive the Arctic climate has treated us to one of its characteristic sudden changes, and the beautiful sunlight we have enjoyed for most of the flight has gone, replaced by thick flakes of snow falling heavily from a cloud-covered sky. As we approach, the lodge building looks incredibly tiny in the vastness of the Arctic tundra. We land in a flurry of snow whipped up by the whirling blades. We are instructed to wait in the helicopter while the area is scanned for polar bears - apparently female bears have visited the immediate area of the lodge several times in the past few days and we would be vulnerable to attack even in the one hundred metre dash between the helicopter and the doorway. A roaming female bear with a cub to feed would be delighted to find a plump snack walking through her homeland - even if she would be a little disappointed to discover that the greatest portion of her intended meal consisted of layers of down-filled clothing.

A female bear and her cub spotted from the helicopter.

We introduce ourselves to our host, Dwight Allen. Dwight grew up in Churchill, and is the manager of the Polar Inn, where we had spent such a comfortable couple of nights. He is based at the lodge for the duration of the migration of the female bears to compile film footage that will be used by wildlife programme makers. He is also researching a study into the bear's vocal communication - apparently very little is known about the bear's calls and their possible meaning.

The lodge is rustic and fairly basic, but unimaginable luxury compared to the accommodation on our last visit to the Arctic. Built in the 1900s it was once the local trading post used by the Inuit, Cree and Chipawa Indian tribes. Later it was the sight of the local brothel! We have gas lighting and heating and a wood-burning stove. The square wooden building consists of one large communal room, boasting a dining table and some ancient squashy sofas - piles of reference books about the ecology and exploration of the Arctic lie around. Doors at each end of this main room open directly to the outside, leading onto wooden decks which we can be used to observe any bears who may visit. Running down the left hand side of the lounge room is a basic, but well-equipped kitchen, doors on the other side lead to dormitory-style bedrooms, with narrow bunk beds. Although the lodge feels comparatively warm, I notice the feathery swirls of hoar frost on the inside of the dormitory windows. I am delighted to find that there is a small bathroom with a sink - and not just one toilet, but two! The reason for this soon becomes clear - the lodge does *not* have separate ladies and gents facilities. As we are staying in an uncontaminated region of natural habitat, all solid waste must be compacted for eventual removal and subsequent disposal in the sewage systems of Churchill.

Our mode of travel.

The entire lodge is enclosed within a huge metal cage. The exterior decks stretch between the wooden walls to the thick steel bars - a distance of at most 2 metres. We will not be able to leave the confines of these few rooms within the cage until the helicopter returns to collect us again in two weeks time. This is a short visit compared to the study periods of some of the students and scientists who use the lodges facilities through the year - a self-imposed imprisonment in a frozen landscape.

White Whale Lodge seen through the blizzard.

We have come to this unique location in the hope of seeing females with cubs - but there is of course one disadvantage over remaining in Churchill. There we could hire a tundra buggy and drive out in search of bears - here we have to wait for them to come to us. In the event, we have been in the lodge less than half an hour when Dwight calls us; he has been filming a one-year-old male polar bear who has been wandering around the area for several days and the bear has returned. We dash out onto the front deck and can hardly believe what we are seeing.

At a year old the bear is perhaps only half the size he will reach when fully grown. He ambles up to the bars, sniffing the air as he approaches. Although he is already capable of running fast enough to cover a mile in two minutes, he is taking his time. Perhaps he knows that we are in no rush to leave. Still a youngster, the pure white fur on his face is unblemished by the scars which mark the older males. He is not yet old enough to join the vicious fights

Our basic but well-equipped kitchen.

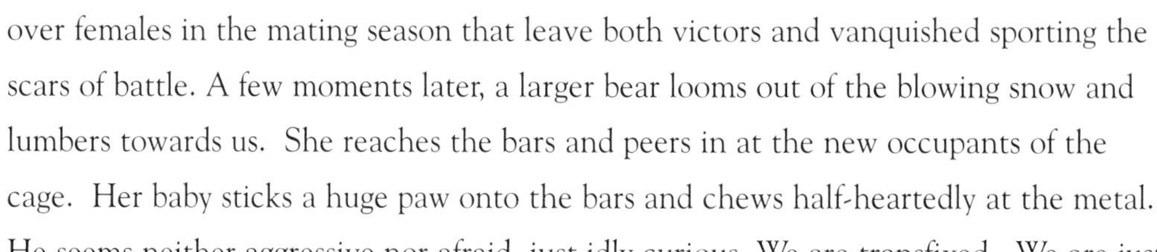

THE BEARS LOOM OUT OF THE BLOWING SNOW.

over females in the mating season that leave both victors and vanquished sporting the scars of battle. A few moments later, a larger bear looms out of the blowing snow and lumbers towards us. She reaches the bars and peers in at the new occupants of the cage. Her baby sticks a huge paw onto the bars and chews half-heartedly at the metal. He seems neither aggressive nor afraid, just idly curious. We are transfixed. We are just feet away from wild bears, as we were in the buggies - but this time we are at ground level with them, and separated only by open metal bars. In an amazing reversal of the usual circumstances, we are trapped inside a metal cage (albeit well equipped!) and the bears are free to wander up and stare at us, inhabitants in a human zoo, before strolling off into the ice and snow.

The female yawns, permitting us a remarkably close view of the purple-black lining of her mouth and her huge ivory teeth, which are powerful enough to crush the skull of a seal in one bite. Dwight tells us that when polar bears meet on the ice they yawn to one another to signal that they mean no harm. Is she trying to tell us that she is just curious, just visiting? There is nothing except willpower preventing us from reaching out and touching the tip of the youngster's nose - other than the very real danger of losing an arm of course. The bears appear gentle and docile even in such close proximity, but they are familiar with the lodge and know from experience that they cannot reach inside the bars. They are also ravenously hungry, swift and deadly predators, who would not miss any opportunity for an easy feed. We are warned not to rest our lenses on the bars to watch for bears through our cameras - the tunnel vision caused by the lens would mean that a previously unseen bear could approach unnoticed from the side and attack before we even realised he was there. At such close quarters I fully appreciate for first time the sheer size of these animals. Viewed from a distance across the ice, even peering down at them from a tundra buggy they appear big enough, but crouching at eye level with the female I realise that she is truly enormous.

THERE IS NOTHING EXCEPT WILLPOWER PREVENTING US FROM REACHING OUT AND TOUCHING THE TIP OF THE YOUNGSTER'S NOSE.

An hour later the polar bears leave us - wandering off into the endless snow and ice. I have already exposed nine rolls of film and Pollyanna's sketchpad is filling with line drawings of the bears. If we continue to have such excellent opportunities to see the wildlife, we will both be out of materials in forty-eight hours.

After lunch, inside the welcome warmth of the lodge, I start to make my way out to bear watch - but the bears beat me to it! I am still pulling on layers of clothing when they arrive, and I end up out on the decking without my down coat, protected only by my windproof black nylon jacket. On the back deck there are two wooden ladders which lead up onto the flat wooden roof of the one-storey building. We can climb up onto the roof in order to take photographs - without the bars of cage - but still be safe from bear attack. Climbing a small wooden ladder in sorrel boots is quite an art - I have enough trouble controlling them when I am walking on flat ground - and my progress up the ladder is slow and tenuous. The view from the top, entirely unadulterated by metal bars, is spectacular - as is the Arctic wind which whips across the exposed roof. Without the protection of the very large purple jacket I feel frozen in no time, the wind blowing into my face, making my eyes stream, but I am rewarded with photographs of the cub rolling and playing in the snow. Pollyanna has sensibly taken the few extra seconds needed to dress properly, and is sitting on the corner of the roof, just the ends of her fingers exposed as she rapidly sketches. Eventually the cold defeats me, and I slither and stumble back down the ladder to thaw out in the lodge, where I can dress properly for the conditions, so that I can return and continue adding to my increasing collection of used films.

Hoar frost on the lodge window.

My photographs will eventually be used to illustrate Pollyanna's lectures. They are, of course, also useful to Pollyanna when she starts work on her paintings - vividly helping to recall a scene or a certain light. A photograph can catch motion - a bird in flight, or any movement too fast to be captured accurately by the human eye. They can also be useful reference points for certain details, such as fur texture, or the actual position of an animal. Film does not always provide an accurate representation of colour and the developing process can have a huge effect on subtle shades and tones. Sometimes, however, wild animals do not obligingly stay around to pose for sketches and a quick snapshot can be the only record we have of a sighting. Although the photographs are undoubtedly a valuable reference for Pollyanna, none of her paintings is ever a slavishly accurate copy of my photographs. As she says, "What would be the point in that? You may as well frame an enlargement." Instead, her paintings evolve from a whole range of inspirations, but primarily her sketches, which are the life blood of her

Between the lodge and the bars.

Mother and year-old cub leave the lodge and trudge back across the ice.

paintings. Although Pollyanna does take some photographs herself, she always prefers to sketch when possible. "Looking through a lens and pressing the shutter takes a fraction of a second, but when I sketch I have to really concentrate and look carefully at my subjects. I feel that it is through this process that I really learn the character of an animal." At the heart of every new painting is her genuine love and respect for wildlife, and lifelong dedication to her art.

White Whale Lodge is set on the northerly shores of the Hudson Bay and to our delight, as we are watching the cub, he dives into the grey water to swim among the slushy ice which is starting to form. In little more than a week this ice will be solidifying, becoming dense pack ice, enabling the bears to leave the area of the lodge and head out in search of seals. Watching his head resurface among the icy waves, we are awed by the way these magnificent animals are so well adapted to this inhospitable habitat and are able to swim in near freezing waters. Despite this his mother does not seem keen to join him, she climbs onto the higher ground of the cliffs, watching her youngster as he clambers out to join her, a spray of water flying from his fur as he shakes his thick coat. The cub then slides down the cliff side on his chest, once at the bottom he rolls onto his back wriggling and squirming in the snow. Dwight tells us that the cub is using this dry snow to absorb the water from his wet coat - instinctively the cub knows fur that remains wet, or becomes too dirty, will not act as an efficient insulator. To survive the extreme cold of the dark winter months a polar bear needs to keep his coat in good condition.

On meeting, yawning to one another signals that they mean no harm.

Our days at the lodge quickly and quietly settle into a routine. We take it in turns to spot bears, dashing outside at the first sighting, then returning to the warmth of the lodge to thaw out when the bear chooses to leave.

Back inside the lodge, Pollyanna continues to work on her sketches, using watercolour washes to bring them to life, catching the subtle shadows of the polar bear's fur, and the crisp cold of the snowy landscapes. Although the sheets of watercolour paper she travels with are relatively small (roughly A3 sheets), once she starts work in her studio she prefers to work on a much larger scale. The finished dimensions of most of her paintings will be over 1 x 1.2 m - inspired by the sweeping vastness of the Arctic landscape and the awe-inspiring polar bears. Back home in England these finished paintings will transport the viewers to a different world, into this far-away land on top of the world.

The lodge boasts a television set (but no television reception) and Dwight is pleased to show us some of the beautiful footage he has shot of both bears and Arctic foxes. Dwight also has a collection of wildlife documentaries and an extremely small library of feature films - to be specific the 1959 epic *The Savage Innocents*, starring both Peter O'Toole and Anthony Quinn - though probably not frequently mentioned with pride by either of them. I suspect that Anthony Quinn probably preferred to try and wipe from his memory (if not from the film archives), the unintentionally humorous scene in which his Inuit wife slaps him in the face with a dead fish. Dwight suggests we may enjoy watching the movie one evening, as it was filmed in an area very close to where the lodge stands. Given the nature of this treeless icy landscape, we have to take his word for this.

Arctic foxes are often seen following polar bears, scavenging the remains of their hunting trips.

Throughout our stay the bears are good to us - we are lucky enough to see one or more each day we remain in the lodge. As well as the mother bear and her yearling cub, who visit frequently, two other adult females decide to view the lodge on their route to the coast. One of the females who visits has obviously had a previous experience of scientific study as she is tagged with a radio collar.

The regular presence of the mother and cub give us an unparalleled opportunity to observe their relationship. Although the cub is growing rapidly into adolescence he rarely strays far from his mother's side. On occasion he will still attempt to suckle. Like the young males we observed in Churchill he is keen to rehearse his fighting skills for the day he will join the other adults in competition for a female. His mother is happy to wrestle with him, rising onto her hind legs, her paws hanging by her side she allows him to push and pull, grappling with him in a slow motion waltz. He pulls her over and they fall into the snow, still grappling and scuffling, he mouths at her

ABOVE AND BELOW:
HIS MOTHER IS HAPPY TO WRESTLE WITH HIM, RISING ONTO HER HIND LEGS, HER PAWS HANGING BY HER SIDE SHE ALLOWS HIM TO PUSH AND PULL, GRAPPLING WITH HIM IN A SLOW MOTION WALTZ.

thick fur, pretending to bite. Both bears are clearly not using even a fraction of their full strength in this mock battle. When the mother bear has had enough just one firm slap from her gigantic paw is enough to bring the game to an end. I can tell that Pollyanna can hardly wait to begin work on paintings of the mother bear and her cub - an opportunity to show in her work the tender if fierce love of this huge animal. This will be in great contrast to her previous works which conveyed the solitary power of the lone male.

To Jason's delight we also see several Arctic foxes and even have the opportunity to watch one of them hunting, just outside the lodge. Stepping delicately over the snow, then abruptly stopping, head cocked to one side, the fox is alert for the sound of lemmings burrowing under the snow cover. Suddenly the fox darts its head forwards, plunging its muzzle into the thick snow, triumphantly rising again moments later with a lemming clutched in its jaws, then trotting briskly off to eat its reward. Jason tells me that the foxes also store food in caches, to support them through the lean winter months. Arctic foxes are often seen following polar bears, scavenging the remains of their hunting trips. Apparently the bears tolerate the foxes quite happily, only swiping them aside with a sweep of a paw if they try to grab the food before the bear has finished eating.

We catch the occasional glimpse of the lemmings (while still out of the mouths of foxes) as they break cover to scurry quickly over the surface snow, before speedily burrowing back underneath.

One morning we are awoken by a commotion in the kitchen - the cub has smelt Dwight's breakfast cooking and stuck his head right through the small window at the back of the kitchen, which was slightly open. There is much commotion as Dwight forces the window shut to repel the intruder. Although the hungry bears must find the smell of toasting muffins irresistible, it is obviously forbidden to feed these wild

Guess who's coming for breakfast?

animals, or in any way to encourage them near the lodge with bait. It would be extremely dangerous to encourage any association of humans and food - and of course we are only there to observe the bears, not make changes to their natural diet, or encourage them to remain in an area which they came to associate with a food source, rather than following their natural migration route.

However, even the best intentions of preserving a pristine environment when we leave can be foiled by hungry bears. All the rubbish generated by the lodge is stored by Dwight in a shed close by and will eventually be flown out by helicopter. Early one morning the cub's natural curiosity overwhelms him and he manages to smash his way through the wooden panels of the wall and drag out a bin bag. The contents prove of little interest, like a young child with a Christmas present he is more interested in the wrapping. The wind whips the bag out of his jaws and he races after it, his heels kicking up the powdery snow. He proudly catches it once again, only to resume his game as it blows across the ice. Dwight has to wait until the coast is clear of bears (quite literally) before he can dash out to repair the damage, and attempt once again to make the shed bear-proof.

The wind whips the bag out of his jaws and he races after it, his heels kicking up the powdery snow.

Towards the end of our stay, we can all feel that the Arctic winter is advancing rapidly. Pack ice is forming at the edge of the bay. Just one more week of sub-zero temperatures will thicken the ice sufficiently for the polar bears to leave the land. The wind has an ever more vicious bite. As the early morning sun rises, a freezing mist floats up from the sea, and 'sun dogs' appear around the sun. Dwight tells us that this effect, which appears as two segments of rainbow encircling the wintry sun, only appears in the extreme cold, the result of light from the sun reflecting and refracting off ice crystals suspended in the air.

When I venture up to the roof to take photographs of this phenomenon, the roof-top thermometer reads –24°C, but the wind chill measures –50°C - twice as cold as the interior of my freezer back home. The phenomenon known as wind chill is caused by the constantly changing air around the body absorbing body heat and thus greatly intensifying the feeling of cold. A fast blowing icy wind transforms a moderate chill into a stinging, bitter

I am hoping that the pictures I am taking are as beautiful as they appear through the lens.

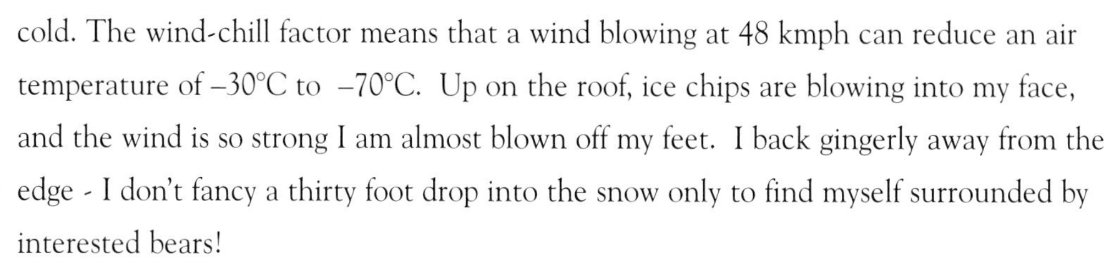

cold. The wind-chill factor means that a wind blowing at 48 kmph can reduce an air temperature of –30°C to –70°C. Up on the roof, ice chips are blowing into my face, and the wind is so strong I am almost blown off my feet. I back gingerly away from the edge - I don't fancy a thirty foot drop into the snow only to find myself surrounded by interested bears!

I am hoping that the pictures I am taking are as beautiful as they appear through the lens - the female and cub are walking towards the lodge from the shoreline, lit by the soft clear morning light. I am wearing photographic mittens, which peel back to become finger-less gloves, leaving my fingers free to operate the cameras. Somehow, knowing I can always retreat back to the warmth of the lodge has lulled me into a false sense of security, and I am underestimating the severity of the Arctic climate in a way I would never have done while travelling by dog sledge, when I was constantly exposed to the elements.

I am underestimating the severity of the Arctic climate.

I become aware that something may be wrong with my right hand, when I attempt to press the shutter release on my camera. I cannot feel my index finger at all. I cannot press the button. I try to press with my middle finger, my ring finger - nothing. All four fingers on my right hand are completely numb. My camera is covered in frost and my fingers are bone white. I stumble back down the ladder to the lodge. A solemn-faced Dwight puts my hand in a bowl of cold water - he fears that I have the very first stages of frost bite. It would be dangerous to try to heat up my fingers too quickly. Eventually, I feel the blood start to return to the tips of my fingers - and with it the pain. Within an hour, the ends of my fingers feel and look as though I have slammed them in a door. There is a constant hot throbbing pain, and my fingers are purple. Within forty-eight hours a thick layer of skin starts to peel off in a very attractive way. Thankfully, however, I realised what was happening and came inside in time and I have not done any permanent damage to my hand - with the exception of a small patch of skin on the very tip of my ring finger which still remains numb. This has been a harsh, but timely, reminder that no matter how beautiful the Arctic light and landscape may seem, the vicious severity of the climate can never be underestimated.

The female and cub are walking towards the lodge from the shoreline.

The Arctic weather has one final trick in store for us. On the morning we are due to be

collected by helicopter and flown back to Churchill, a wild snow storm is blowing. Dwight radios through to the pilot; the weather in Churchill is clear and bright, but he cannot fly into the storm. We have flights back to Winnipeg booked first thing the following morning and if we cannot leave the lodge by nightfall, we will not be able to reach the plane in time. A day of waiting and watching the weather follows, while Dwight keeps up regular radio contact.

Eventually, the storm subsides enough to allow the helicopter to fly in and Pollyanna, Jason and I clamber aboard. The helicopter lifts and we watch the lodge vanish below us in a flurry of white, locked into a snowy wasteland for the duration of the Arctic winter.

We spend our last night in Churchill back in the Polar Inn. We walk to the nearby Tundra Inn for an evening meal. When we leave to return to the hotel the skies are clear and as we walk back down the icy pavement the first unmistakable chiffon wisps of the colours of the Northern Lights start to appear. They are directly overhead, sweeping and swirling across the sky and rapidly strengthening in intensity. We are transfixed. Churchill is an ideal location to view the Aurora Borealis, as it lies under the region of the highest intensity of auroral activity in the Arctic. However, we were not visiting at the ideal time of year, and as the weather has been frequently overcast, had held little hope of witnessing this most spectacular display of nature's beauty. A truck pulls up alongside us. Jason is driving, with Hugh, another member of the Natural Habitats team - they are heading out of the town onto the tundra to view the lights in all their magical glory. We climb in and rattle our way out though the icy streets of the town. I had always imagined the Northern Lights would appear as a far off display on the horizon, very beautiful, but viewed like a projection onto a very distant cinema screen. When we climb out of the truck, away from the light pollution of the town, the lights are directly overhead, curtains of pale fire rippling through the diamond clear sky in a myriad of chasing colours and patterns. Even Jason and Hugh, who have often seen the Aurora Borealis, are rendered speechless by this particularly vivid and remarkable display arching overhead. The four of us turn slow circles on the ice, unaware of the bitingly cold Arctic air, occasionally uttering an entirely inadequate "Wow!". The Norwegian explorer Fridtjof Nansen called the Aurora 'The Symphony of Eternity', a much more poetic and evocative description of this breathtaking display.

**FROSTBITE**

**In the most basic terms, frostbite occurs when the skin and/or the tissue under the skin freezes and causes cell damage. This is caused by exposure to cold air (and in other circumstances through chemical exposure) and under extreme conditions can happen in seconds. When exposed to the cold the blood vessels constrict, restricting flow to the extremities (fingers, toes, nose, etc.). This is a natural reaction to prevent heat loss and hypothermia. The fluid within the cells and tissues starts to freeze and form ice crystals. The crystals take up more room in the cells than when in a fluid state and thus cause the cells to rupture. There are three levels of severity. First-degree frostbite (sometimes called frost nip) presents itself as numbed skin which has turned white in colour. The skin feels stiff to the touch, but the tissue underneath is still warm and soft. There is very little risk of blistering or scarring. In second-degree frostbite the skin will be blue or white and will feel hard and frozen. Although the tissue underneath remains undamaged, blistering is likely and proper medical attention should be sought. In third-degree, or deep frostbite, the skin is white, blotchy or blue and the tissue underneath is hard and cold to the touch. This is a life-threatening condition. Blistering will happen and in severe cases the extremities will be lost.**

Other vehicles draw up, and we realise that even some of the town's inhabitants have driven out to gaze up at the constantly changing curtains of swirling lights which move across the heavens, folding and turning, fading away then intensifying and flaring brightly once again. The Canadian Inuit believed the spectral dance was the souls of the dead at play in the heavens, watching the glowing diaphanous colours casting their spectral light on the snows, this does not seem too fanciful. The night seems filled with magic, and I have the romantic notion that the polar bears out on the tundra pause to gaze at the phosphorus green and violet swathes of phantom light curling and streaking against the starlit Arctic sky.

It is only when the spectacle is finally fading, and Jason is driving us back into town, that I realise I never once thought of my camera.

The following morning we leave Churchill and this land of eternal ice and snow behind us once again. It is hard to imagine that any place exists which is less hospitable to life, yet we have been drawn here a second time by the lure of the great white bear, so at home in the cruelly magnificent beauty of this wilderness.

A career spanning thirty years, devoted to art and nature and filled with rapid sketching and painting from memory, has rewarded Pollyanna with an almost photographic recollection of colour and atmosphere. Her first painting, inspired by her experiences along Hudson Bay, would be of a lone male polar bear. Pausing in his long nomadic trek across the ice, he gazes in wonder, just as we did, at one of the world 's most beautiful natural spectacles - the Northern Lights dancing through the night skies on top of the world.

THE END

**THE NORTHERN LIGHTS**

**In 1621 French scientist Pierre Gassandi observed the Dancing Lights in the Northern Skies, and named them 'Aurora' after the Roman goddess of the dawn. He added 'Borea' from the name of the Bores, the Roman god of the north winds. This poetic name beautifully describes a remarkable natural phenomenon. The earth's atmosphere, which stretches hundreds of miles above the planet's surface, contains many gases, chiefly nitrogen and oxygen. The earth acts as an enormous magnet, pulling particles from the sun towards the skies above its magnetic poles. Simplistically, the Aurora Borealis occurs when high-speed particles from the sun strike the gases swirling in the atmosphere, making them glow.**

Photograph
© Bryan and Cherry Alexander

Pollyanna Pickering

# THE PAINTINGS

*'When I travel I am able to experience the natural world in all its beauty, danger and drama. It is only through this first-hand study of animals and their habitats that I am able to paint in a way that communicates my love and respect for our remarkable, awe-inspiring but ultimately fragile world.'*

POLLYANNA PICKERING

On Top of the World

*'I try in vain to be persuaded that the pole is the seat of frost and desolation, it ever presents itself to my imagination as the region of beauty and delight. There ... the sun is forever visible; its broad disk just skirting the horizon, and diffusing a perpetual splendour. There ... snow and frost are banished; and, sailing over a calm sea, we may be wafted to a land surpassing in wonders and in beauty every region hitherto discovered on the habitable globe ... What may not be expected in a country of eternal light?'*

MARY SHELLEY (*FRANKENSTEIN*) 1818

ARCTIC MIDNIGHT
IN THE COLLECTION OF ANNA-LOUISE PICKERING (UK)

*'There's a blueness to this place. A very pale azure blue. It's startling. It's the ice under the snow, this ice which is the most spectacular blue. It's bluer than your old faded Levis, just blue, blue of the bluest eyes. Blue, blue, blue, blue. I sound, I know, a bit airy fairy. A bit like some limp-wristed old water-colour painter, but it is, let me tell you, it's a bit good!'*

BILLY CONNOLLY
*A SCOT IN THE ARCTIC*

ARCTIC ROLL

*'Wandering re-establishes the original harmony which once existed between man and the universe.'*

ANATOLE FRANCE

The Sound of Silence

Two Below Zero

*'Come forth into the light of things*
*Let nature be your teacher.'*

WILLIAM WORDSWORTH

*'I think again over my small Adventures*
*My Fears*
*Those small ones seemed so big*
*For all the vital things*
*I had to get and reach*
*And yet there is only one great thing*
*The Only thing*
*To live and see the great day that dawns*
*The light that fills the world.'*

TRADITIONAL INUIT SONG

Child of the Arctic
In the collection of Mr and Mrs M Askew (UK)

*'The polar bear is a noble looking animal and of enormous strength, living bravely and warm amid eternal ice ... they are the unrivalled master-existences of this icebound solitude.'*

JOHN MUIR, AMERICAN NATURALIST IN NORTHERN CANADA, 1881

Bear Hug

*'And now there came both mist and snow*
*And it grew wondrous cold:*
*And ice mast high came floating by,*
*As green as emerald.*

*The ice was here, the ice was there,*
*The ice was all around:*
*It cracked and growled, and roared*
*and howled,*
*Like noises in a swound!'*

SAMUEL TAYLOR COLERIDGE
*THE RIME OF THE ANCIENT MARINER*

Ice Age

*'That country is so cold for seven or eight months of the year, that the sea freezes ten feet deep, the trees and the very stones split, the snow is ten or twelve feet deep upon the ground, for above six months of the year, and during that season, no body can stir out of doors without running the risk of having their nose, ears, and feet mortified by the cold.'*

BARON DE LA HONTAN, FRENCH TRAVELLER,
*NEW VOYAGES TO NORTH AMERICA*, 1682 - 1694

The Blizzard

. . . And in Winter the Sea Freezes Over

*'I never found the companion that was so companionable as solitude.'*

HENRY DAVID THOREAU, 1854

## *The Inuit Year*

*'The season of light and the season*
*of darkness*
*The season of baby seals and*
*the season of the caribou hunt*
*The season of running char and the*
*season of the denning polar bear*
*The season of the igloo and the season*
*of the skin tent*
*The season of the geese nesting and*
*the season of berries.'*

TRADITIONAL INUIT POEM

One Man and his Dog
in the collection of Mrs B. Garthwaite (UK)

*'We must see beyond textbooks, go out into the by-paths and untrodden depths of the wilderness and travel and explore and tell the world the glories of our journey'*

WALTER BAUER

In the Land of the Midnight Sun

*'We do not receive wisdom, we must discover it for ourselves, after a journey through the wilderness which no one else can make for us, which no one can spare us, for our wisdom is the point of view from which we come at last to regard the world.'*

MARCEL PROUST

A Very Safe Place to Be
Private collection (UK)

*'Take the breath of the new dawn*
*and make it part of you.*
*It will give you strength'*

HOPI INDIAN SAYING

Double Trouble

*'The artist's world is limitless.*
*It can be found anywhere -*
*far from where he lives,*
*or a few feet away.'*

Paul Strand

Cold Comfort

*'Let us permit nature to take her own way, she better understands her own affairs than we'*

MONTAIGNE

Arctic Baby

In the collection of Mr and Mrs Pheasant (UK)

*'Our first polar bear moved past us on the floes with the leisurely march of fearless freedom ... he never varied from his unconcerned walk. We saw him last in a labyrinth of hummock ice.'*

Dr Kent Kane describes his first encounter with a polar bear in his journal of the *US Grinnell* Expedition

Kingdom of the Ice Bear

*'The Arctic expresses the sum of all wisdom; silence'*

Walter Bauer

The Dream of the White Bear

*'Look deep into nature, and then you will understand all things better.'*

ALBERT EINSTEIN

CIRCLE OF LIFE
PRIVATE COLLECTION (UK)

*'Thank God! there is always a land of beyond*
*For those who are true to the trail*
*A vision to seek, a beckoning peak*
*A farness that never will fail'*

Robert Service
Yukon poet

Where the North Wind doth Blow

Pollyanna Pickering at work in the warmth of her studio.

# Afterword

This book is intended as a personal account of the experiences of two English women discovering the realities of Arctic life. We travelled up to the Arctic independently in order to allow Pollyanna to study and paint the unique wildlife of one of the few remaining wildernesses on our planet.

We did not have any connection with scientific or charitable organisations, and were not attempting any scientific or exploratory studies. Although I have endeavoured to research as carefully as possible any information which is included about polar bears, new studies are providing fresh facts and figures on a regular basis and I apologise for any inaccuracies.

Our greatest hope is that mankind will leave this unique environment unexploited and unpolluted so that the remarkable Arctic ecosystem will remain to provide inspiration and wonder for many more millennia. Through her remarkable paintings of polar bears, Pollyanna hopes to bring people's attention to animals they may never encounter first hand, but whose very existence is irrevocably linked to ours in the grand scheme of the natural world.

*'We were not pioneers ourselves, but we journeyed over*
*old trails that were new to us, and with hearts open. Who shall distinguish?'*

J. Monroe Thorington
*The Glittering Mountains of Canada*

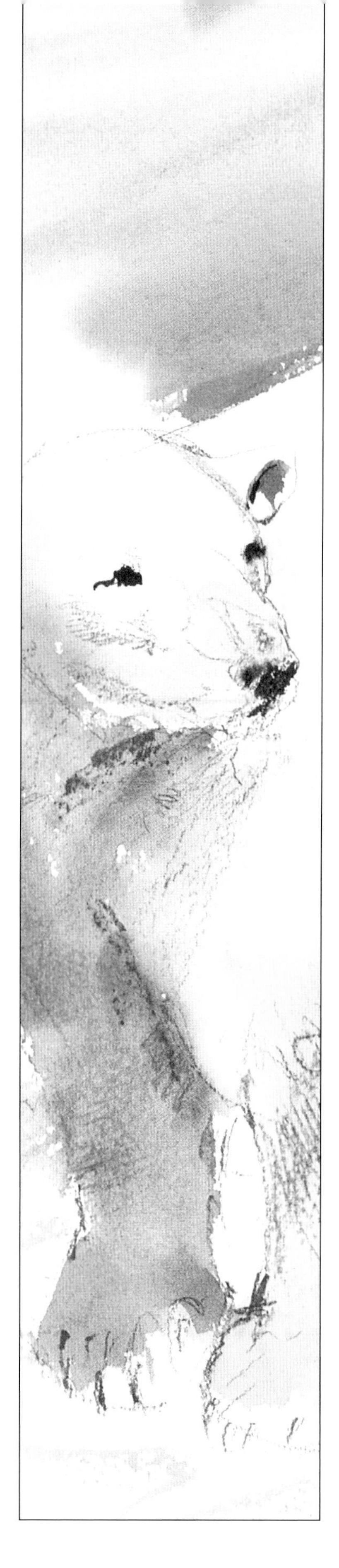

# Bibliography


Thor Larsen, *The World of the Polar Bear:* Chartwell Books Inc, 1978

Bernard Stonehouse, *North Pole South Pole (A Guide to the Ecology and Resources of the Arctic and Antarctic)*: Prion, 1990

Fred Bruemmer and Brian Davies, *Seasons of the Seal:* Key Porter Books, 1988

Keith Shackleton, *Wildlife and Wilderness an Artist's World:* Clive Holloway Books, 1986

Dave Taylor, *Ontario's Wildlife:* The Boston Mills Press, 1988

Hugh Miles and Mike Salisbury, *The Kingdom of the Ice Bear:* Guild Publishing, 1985

Brian and Cherry Alexander, *The Vanishing Arctic:* Blandford, 1996

Robert Swan, *Icewalk:* Jonathan Cape, 1990

Downs Matthews, *Polar Bear:* Chronicle Books, 1993

David Mech, *Wolves of the High Arctic:* Voyager Press, 1992

Fred Bruemmer, *World of the Polar Bear:* Bloomsbury, 1989

Robert R Taylor, *The Edge of the Arctic:* Windermere House Publishing, 1992

Norbert Rosing, *The World of the Polar Bear:* Firefly Books, 1996

Lorraine E Brandson, *Carved from the Land:* Eskimo Museum Publishing, 1994

Plus a wide selction of magazine articles, notably:

David Jones, *The Last Roar of The White Bear: Daily Mail,* 03.10.1988

Keith Nyitray, *Alone Across the Arctic Crown: National Geographic,* April 1993

Naomi Uemure, *Solo to the Pole: National Geographic,* September 1978

Nic Fleming, *Natural World in Crisis: The Daily Express,* 09.12.1999

Julian Borger, *World's Climate on Thin Ice, The Times,* 18.11.1999

Alexandra Williams, *We're on Thin Ice as the North Pole Melts, The Daily Mirror,* 21.08.2000

Will Steger, *North To the Pole, National Geographic,* September 1986

Jean Louis Etienne, *Skiing Alone to the Pole, National Geographic,* September 1986

## Acknowledgements

Our first thanks must go to our Inuit guides Gideon and Pakka for returning us safely to Igloolik after our first expedition. Also to Luccassee for all his help during our stay in the village, all at Canada North outfitting, and to Vanessa Janion of Arctic Experience for her advice and help with the travel arrangements. Our return journey would not have happened without the organisational skills of Greg at Natural Habitats. A big thank you to Dwight Allen for welcoming us to the White Whale Lodge, and to all the new friends we made in Churchill including Doris Olson, Dolores Pritchard, Jurgen and Marianne Ludwig, Barbara Balan, Kier and Bertina Boyd, Marjie Willoughby, and Wolfgang and Ursula Stock. Special thanks to Jason for teaching us the night time call of the Arctic fox (just kidding!) and everyone else who assisted with our travels. We remain full of admiration for the wonderful work done by Kay and Larry McKeever at the O.R.R.F., and full of thanks for their hospitality.

Back in England, Gary Beck and all at Otter House who have provided constant encouragement and support during the long process of creating the book. Sue Stainton has once again brought our ideas to life with her wonderful and inspired ideas for layout and design, and Rosemary Lee has shown constant dedication working with her to bring the text, photographs and paintings together into a real book. Thank you again to Alyson Gregory for her patient and thoughtful editing, and to Carrie Thorpe for her exceptional help and research, Peninsular Repro have gone beyond the call of duty in their many overnight vigils scanning and proofing. Special thanks to Andrew Marshall, Steve and Elaine Naylor, Linda and John Soto for all their support.